KNITTED LETTERS

KNITTED LETTERS

Make Personalized Gifts and Accents with Creative Typography-Based Projects

Catherine Hirst and Erssie Major

CHRONICLE BOOKS
SAN FRANCISCO

First published in the United States of America in 2013 by Chronicle Books LLC.

Library of Congress Cataloging-in-Publication Data available.

ISBN 978-1-4521-1572-6

Manufactured in China

Text: Catherine Hirst
Colorwork charts: Erssie Major
Project designers: Claire Crompton, Liz Gregory, Catherine Hirst, Meghan Fernandes, Erssie Major, Carol Meldrum
Designer: Anna Gatt
Photographer: Lydia Evans
Art Director: Michael Charles
Editorial Director: Donna Gregory
Publisher: Mark Searle

10 9 8 7 6 5 4 3 2 1

Chronicle Books
680 Second Street
San Francisco, California 94107
www.chroniclebooks.com

Contents

Introduction

In a vase full of knitting needles on my studio table, I have a pair of casein needles that belonged to my grandmother. She was the one who taught me to knit and crochet, and even though she's been gone for more than twenty years, every time I pick up my needles I feel like I'm communing with her and with all the women in my family who practiced these arts in generations past. I make the same motions and create the same stitches as my grandmother and her mother before her did.

I've knitted (or crocheted) nearly every day of my life since my grandmother first taught me at age seven, and now I teach other people how to do these crafts. I feel like I'm putting just a tiny bit of good back into the world every time someone comes away from a lesson with a newfound understanding of how to wield these sticks and string and—magically!—make garments, accessories, and beautiful things for their home.

Often I'm trying to communicate something with my knitting, which is why I was attracted to this project. I loved the idea of being able to incorporate words and messages into my knitting and customize various projects to my exact specifications. The charts that have been designed for this book are remarkable: Clearly readable when translated into knitting, they are easy to follow and really do impart the essence of each font style that's being celebrated.

Knitting is a traditional means of communication, much like the oral tradition of storytelling that predated the emergence of written language, the printing press, and movable type. This book presents a union of typography and knitting, combining a relatively modern means of communication with a traditional craft that was passed down orally from parent to child for over a thousand years—there are examples of knitted socks from Egypt dating to circa 1000 CE.

I hope that *Knitted Letters* will act as both a resource and an inspiration for incorporating professional-looking typography into your knitting projects. This book contains colorwork charts for nine different typeface styles and also gives instructions for twenty-four knitting projects. Guidance is also given on how to personalize your knitting with your own chosen letters and words, using evenly proportioned and spaced characters to achieve effective, polished results. By providing and demonstrating well-designed typography in yarn form, this book will help you expand your knitting design palette beyond what you ever thought possible.

Using letters and words in your knitting is the ideal means of personalizing your projects, either as gifts for a loved one or as a stylish treat for yourself. The Baby Blanket (page 81) and Neckerchief (page 84) projects both make ideal personalized gifts. Using letters in knitting also means that you can create fun and attractive toys, such as the Alphabet Baby Blocks (page 49), and add novelty to more practical items, like the Felted Pencil Case (page 35).

By illustrating more decorative and elaborate typeface styles such as Script (page 120) and Circus (page 126), this book invites you to explore the possibilities of using letters and characters as decorative elements in their own right—for example, in the Mobius Twist Scarf (page 78). One of the central design problems typographers face when designing a font is the complex trade-off between attractiveness and decoration on the one hand and the clarity and utility of the typeface on the other. Elements such as serifs, and the variation of line thickness within a given character, can aid the reader in following the flow of a word or sentence; equally, an ornate font, which is initially difficult to make out, can arrest the reader's attention and give a specific aesthetic impression. Similarly, with knitting, using an edging, mirrored decreases, or even a specific finishing technique can all change the overall effect of the piece. In *Knitted Letters* you are given all the tools you need to make effective style choices for your knitted projects.

Knitting as a Form of Communication

"(Knitting) is such a communication-based tradition. Knitting is generally done by someone for somebody . . ."

David Revere McFadden, chief curator at the Museum of Arts and Design, New York, on the exhibition *Radical Lace and Subversive Knitting*, 2007

The history of knitting as a form of communication is long and varied, from specific instances of knitting codes or secret messages, to the more general idea of knitting as an art form that brings people together. Whether a knitter is making a blanket for a newborn baby as an expression of love, or yarn-bombing a bicycle rack to bring a burst of color and creativity to the neighborhood, that knitter is sending a message to others. In this way, knitting is similar to typography, and the purpose of this book is to combine the two so that knitters can use their work as a personalized means of expression.

In Charles Dickens's *A Tale of Two Cities*, the character Madame DeFarge knits, in a secret code, a hit list of the names of the aristocrats who will be condemned to death in the French Revolution. Other textiles arts, such as quilting, embroidery, and cross-stitch, have also been used to conceal hidden messages. These days, textile artists are experimenting with incorporating binary and Morse codes into knitting. Knitting is binary, in that it consists of only two stitches—knit and purl. Using simple sequencing, a message can be hidden in a piece of knitting that only someone who knows the secret key can decode. As these examples demonstrate, the ability to transmit information is intrinsic to knitting, and the use of typography in knitting patterns is only one of several ways of communicating with stitches.

When knitting letters and words, the knitter communicates through choices of font, color, and words. The sweet cursive script featured in the Girl's Dress project (page 75) communicates an air of soft femininity, while the bold, sans serif font on the "STOP" Sign Doorstop (page 29) is chosen specifically for clarity and readability. One font is primarily decorative, the other utilitarian. The idea is that each typeface featured within this book is appropriate for different types of knitted projects, so you can customize the project not just with literal words, but also with choices of style.

A compromise often needs to be reached to balance utilitarian functions with the desired decorative flourishes and the piece's overall attractiveness. Perhaps the fundamental difficulty in both knitting and typography design is the trade-off between decoration and utility—striving for beauty while maintaining legibility—and designing letter charts specifically for knitting presents its own set of challenges. Erssie Major, the designer who worked on all the beautiful colorwork charts in this book, had to ensure that the charts were both clear and as small as possible in order to fit onto knitted projects, that they fit knit proportions exactly (since knitted stitches are wider than they are tall), and that they included enough fine detailing to give each typeface a clear and distinct character.

There are fonts from many typeface categories included in the book, such as serif, sans serif, script, slab serif, and black letter. We hope you enjoy creating custom projects of your own and make use of the complete alphabet charts for every font included in the back of the book. Thank you for reading, and happy knitting!

Creating and Customizing Your Own Charts

You can personalize the projects in the book using your own words and letters—don't feel tied to the ones used in the sample projects. Generally speaking, the lettering is incorporated into the projects at a point where the stitch number is stable (i.e., no increasing or decreasing). Therefore, in order to substitute other letters for the chosen ones in the sample, simple arithmetic is all that is required. This is much easier than it sounds.

Let's take the "Amour" Heart Pillow as an example. This project has its lettering positioned in the center of the row within the plain rows of knitting, after the increases from the bottom point. The total number of stitches at that plain knitting section is 97.

For "amour," the width of the charted "a" is 11 stitches, "m" 17 stitches, "o" 9 stitches, "u" 11 stitches, and "r" 11 stitches, for a total width of 59 stitches. There aren't any spaces between the script letters, so the total remains 59.

So, 97 total stitches minus 59 stitches for the charted lettering equals 38 remaining stitches, or 19 plain stitches on either side of the chart (remaining 38 stitches divided by 2 is 19 stitches).

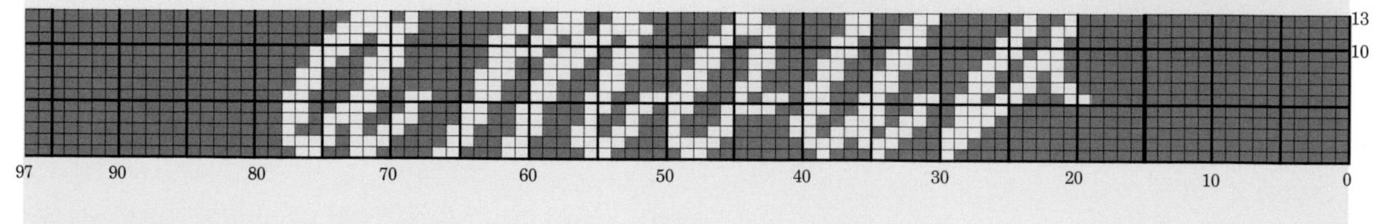

If the word "love" were to be substituted for "amour," then the Script Lowercase Charts (pages 124–25) show that the charted "l" is 14 stitches, "o" 9 stitches, "v" 9 stitches, and "e" 9 stitches, which would make a total of 41 stitches for the lettering. However, the height and forward lean of the "l" means that its top half needs to overlap the "o" above it. Having tried different spacing options, I found that the spacing looked best when the top right edge of the "l" overlapped the left edge of the "o" by 5 stitches, with a 1 stitch space between the foot of the "l" and the "o." In this configuration, the lettering is 36 stitches wide.

Ninety-seven stitches (the width of the pillow at the point where the lettering is positioned) minus 36 is 61, and 61 divided by 2 is an awkward 30½. So to chart "love," there must be 31 plain stitches on the left side of the chart, and 30 on its right side. Often, if your lettering occupies an uneven number of stitches but is centered on a charted section that is an even number of stitches wide, or vice versa, then the space on one side will need to be 1 stitch wider than the space on the other side. In most cases this will be imperceptable, but you may want to try out different options to see what works best.

When making your own charts for different words using different typefaces, you will likely need to go through a similar process of trial and error, moving letters around to get the spacing looking exactly right. This is part of the challenge—while the spacing between most letters can be even and straightforward, some letters are more difficult to get looking exactly right. There is not necessarily a "correct" spacing: If the arrangement of letters and the space between them looks right, then it is right.

Row numbers would need to be adjusted in the same way, depending on the height of the chosen letters. The letters in "amour" are all exactly the same height (13 rows) but the "l" in "love" is taller—twice as tall, in fact, 26 rows.

As with everything, this kind of challenge in knitting becomes easier with practice. Remember, yarn is reusable if you make a mistake!

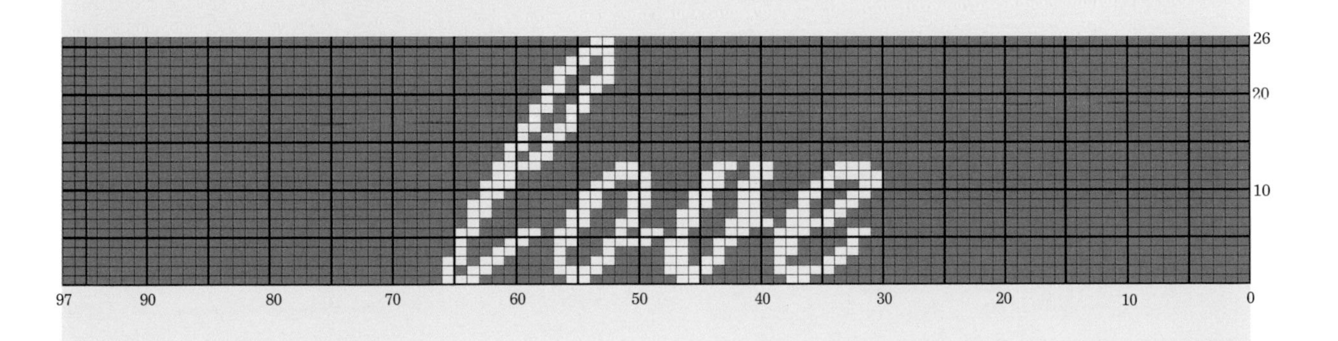

Equipment

All you really need to get started is a pair of knitting needles and some yarn, but depending on your skill level and the complexity of the project, you may need some additional equipment.

Knitting needles—straight

As the popularity of knitting has grown, so has the range of needles. The most common types are plastic, metal, bamboo, and birch wood. They come in different sizes which work with different thicknesses of yarn.

The sizes quoted in the pattern instructions are a useful guide, but you might need to alter the size to achieve the correct fabric gauge. If your gauge is too slack, the project will be too big; if it's too tight, the result will be too small and will also use more yarn.

Knitting needles—double-pointed

Double-pointed needles come in sets of four or five and are generally used for creating smaller projects in the round, but they can also be used to work single-row stripes and to create I-cords.

Needle gauge

A needle gauge is very useful for checking or converting needle sizes, especially as the numbers printed on the needles can wear off with age.

Stitch holder

Stitch holders are used to hold stitches that you are not working with, rather than keeping them on your needles. If you are caught without a stitch holder you can always use a contrasting color of yarn—slip the yarn through the stitches and knot the ends together.

Safety pins

A coiless safety pin can be used as stitch holder if only a few stitches need to be held, or as a stitch marker if you don't have any on hand. They also come in handy if you need to catch a dropped stitch.

Row counter

A row counter fits neatly on the end of a knitting needle. Turn the dial as you work each row.

Stitch marker

Colored plastic or metal rings, stitch markers are useful for marking stitches or rows.

Pins

Glass-headed rustproof dressmaking pins are the best type to use. Pins with brightly colored heads are easy to see against the fabric.

Tape measure/ruler

Choose a tape measure and a clear plastic ruler that show both inches and centimeters.

Scissors

Scissors are an essential part of the kit, and it is best to have several pairs for different uses.

Graph paper/stationery

Graph paper is essential to enable you to trace and draw out your colorwork chart using the charts supplied on pages 108–139. You'll also need all the obvious stationery—pens, pencils, and erasers.

Wool/darning needle

Use a blunt-ended darning needle with a large eye to weave in ends and stitch pieces together.

Reading a Pattern

There is certain information contained in every written pattern, and it is important that you read through the entire pattern before starting to knit any project to ensure that you understand all the abbreviations. Yarn amounts, needle sizes, and any extra equipment and materials will also appear at the beginning of each pattern.

Abbreviations

The patterns in this book feature a number of standard abbreviations, which are explained below.

alt	alternate
beg	begin(s)/beginning
BO	bind off
CC	contrasting color
ch	chain
CO	cast on
cont	continue
dec(s)	decrease(s)/ decreasing
DPN(s)	double-pointed needle(s)
inc(s)	increase(s)
k	knit
k2tog	knit 2 stitches together (decrease 1)
k2togtbl	knit 2 stitches together through the back loop (decrease 1)
k1f&b	knit into front and back loop of same stitch (increase 1 st)
LH	left hand
M1	make 1 stitch
MC	main color
p	purl
p1f&b	purl into the front and back loop of same stitch (increase 1)
p2tog	purl 2 stitches together (decrease 1)
p2togtbl	purl 2 stitches together through back loop (decrease 1)
patt	pattern(s)
pfb	purl into front and back loop of same stitch
prev	previous(ly)
rem	remain/remaining
rep	repeat(s)
RH	right hand
rnd(s)	round(s)
RS	right side
sc	single crochet
sl st	slip stitch
skpo	slip 1 knitwise, knit 1, pass the slipped stitch over (decrease 1)
ssk	slip, slip, knit (decrease 1)
st(s)	stitch(es)
st st	stockinette stitch
tbl	through back loop
tog	together
WS	wrong side
WSF	wrong side facing
*	repeat from *

Techniques

Gauge

Most knitting patterns specify an ideal gauge, which is the number of stitches and rows counted over a specific measurement, usually 4 in/ 10 cm square. If your gauge is not correct, the knitting will end up the wrong size. This is not important for some projects, but it is crucial to get the gauge right when knitting something that is going to be worn, such as a hat or gloves.

Making a test swatch

Cast on the number of stitches given in the gauge guide plus 4 more. If the stitches are to be measured over a pattern, cast on the correct multiple of stitches for the pattern. Work in the required pattern until the swatch measures approx. 5 in/12 cm. Break off the yarn, slip it through the stitches and slip off the needle—you don't have to bind off, as this can distort the stitches.

Counting stitches and rows

Lay the swatch down on a flat surface, and in the center place a ruler horizontally on the square. Place a pin at one point and another 4 in/10 cm away. Count the stitches between the pins, including any half stitches. Repeat the process vertically to count the rows. Remember to count accurately, as even half a stitch could make a difference to the finished size.

Adjusting gauge

If you have fewer stitches than specified, your swatch is too loose and the garment will be too big. Work up another swatch with a smaller needle.

If you have more stitches than specified, your swatch is too tight and the garment will be too small. Work up another swatch with a bigger needle.

Making a Slipknot

A knitted fabric is made by working rows of stitches in various sequences. In order to create a fabric, you must first make a base row, known as a cast-on row. A slipknot is used as the first stitch for a cast-on row.

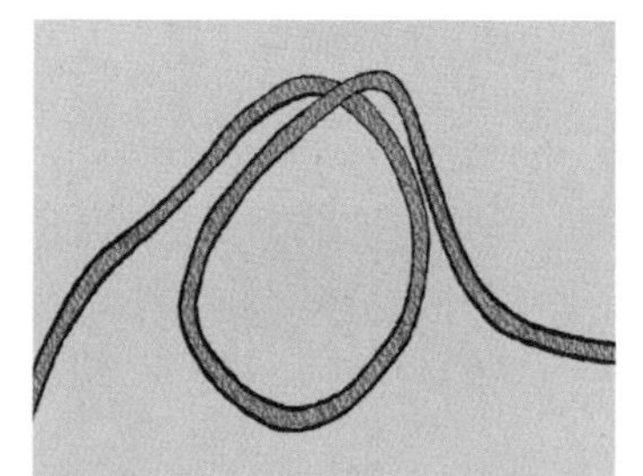

1 Holding the yarn in both hands, make a small loop in the yarn. Take the piece that you are holding in the right hand underneath the loop.

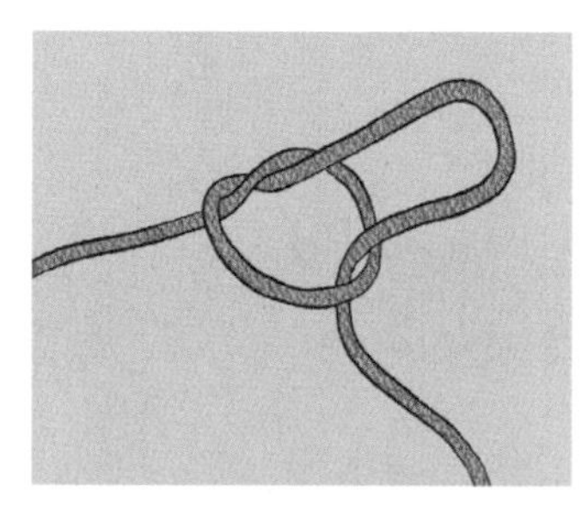

2 Pull this piece of yarn through the original loop to create a knot. Do not pull the short end of the yarn through the loop. Place the slipknot onto the knitting needle.

Casting On

Casting on is the first step in hand knitting and it provides the first row of loops on the needle. Different methods of casting on produce different types of edges. The diagrams below show the cable method, but if you are familiar with another method, you can use that instead.

The cable method

This cast-on method uses both knitting needles and creates a firm edge.

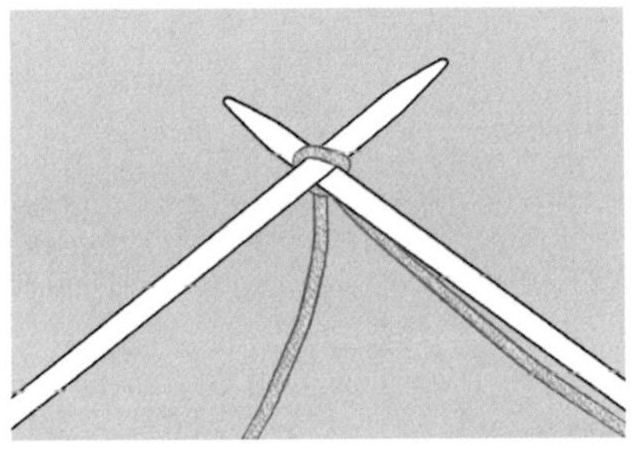

1 Place the slipknot onto the knitting needle and hold the needle in your left hand. Slide the right knitting needle through the loop created by the slipknot from front to back.

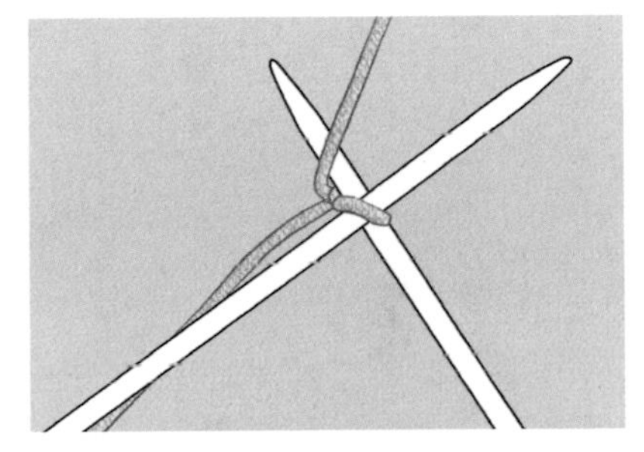

2 With your right hand, wrap the yarn around the right knitting needle counterclockwise from back to front.

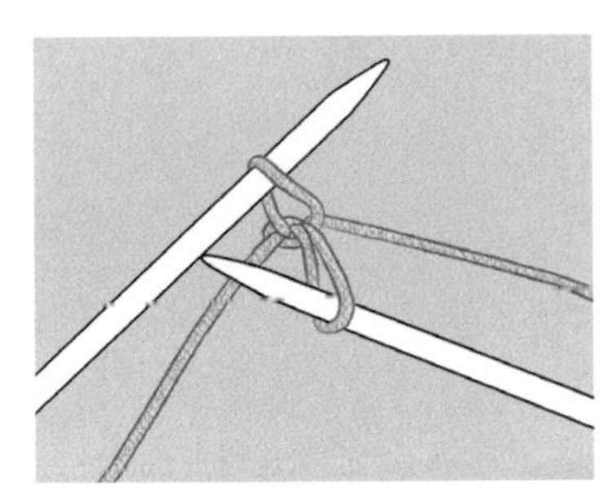

3 Slide the right needle through the loop on the left needle, catching the wrapped yarn and bringing it through the loop to create a new loop.

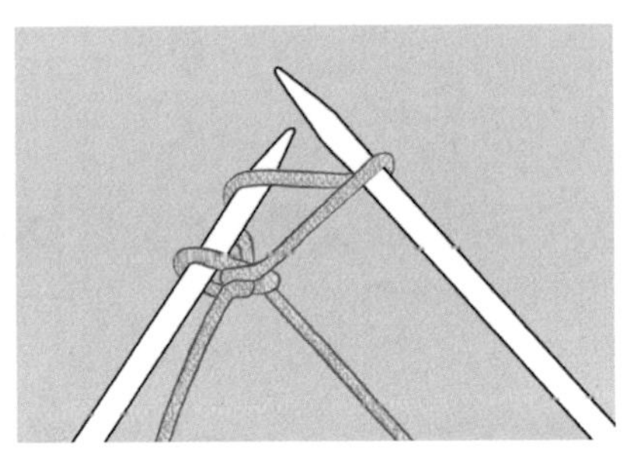

4 Pass the left needle over the top of the new loop, placing the tip of the needle through the loop on the right needle. Remove the right needle, thus transferring the stitch to the left needle.

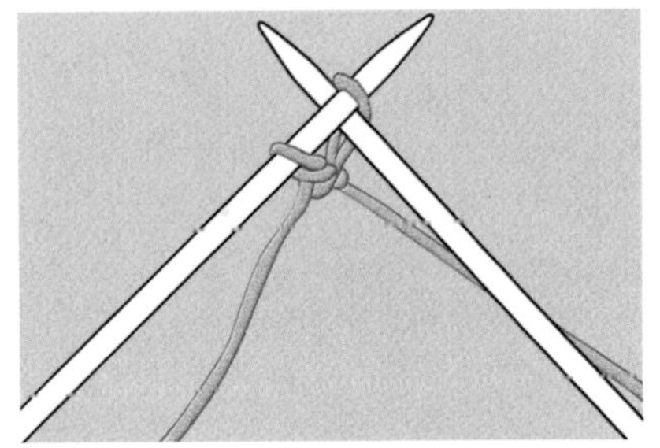

5 Make each subsequent stitch by placing the right needle between the last 2 stitches made on the left needle, and repeating steps 2 through 4.

Binding Off

There is one simple and commonly used method of securing stitches once you have finished a piece of knitting known as "binding off." The most common—the cable bind-off—is shown below.

These diagrams show binding off along a knit row. However, you can bind off in pattern along any fabric, by working each stitch as set in pattern.

Cable bind-off

Cable bind-off is worked using the two needles you have been working with all along.

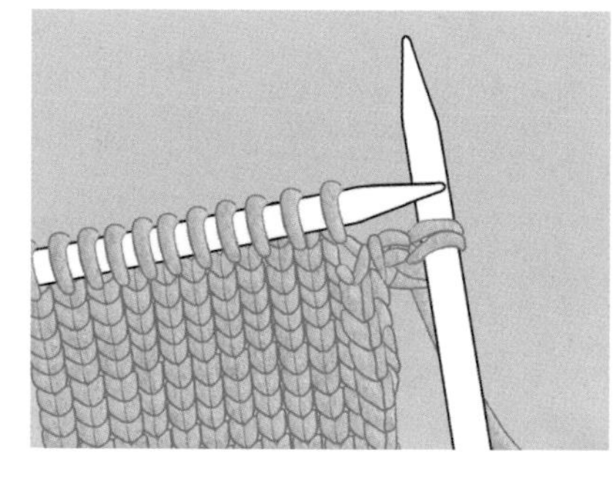

1 When you are ready to bind off, knit the first 2 stitches.

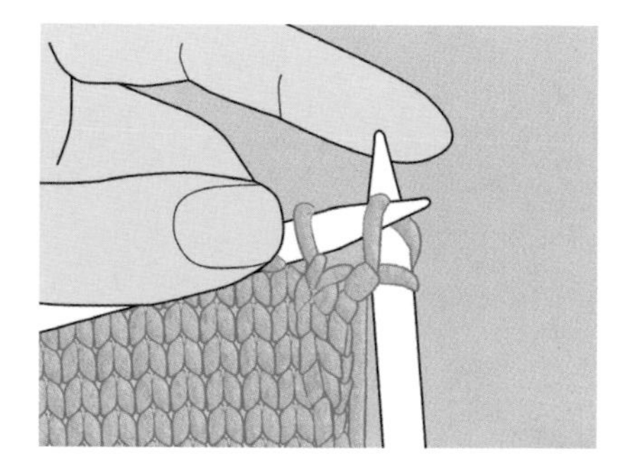

2 Slip the left-hand needle into the first stitch on the right-hand needle, and lift it over the second stitch and off the needle.

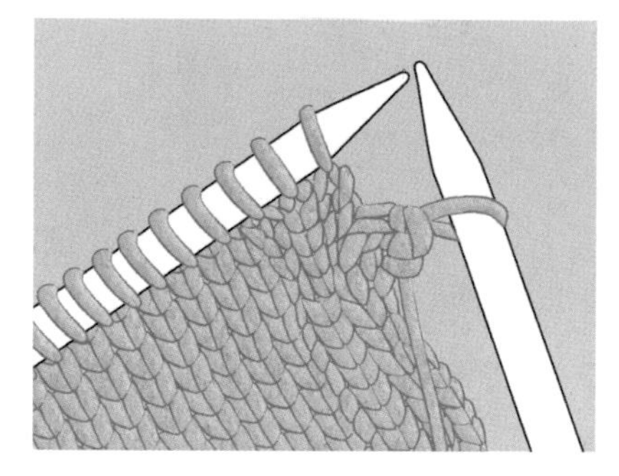

3 Knit the next stitch so that there are 2 stitches on the right-hand needle again.

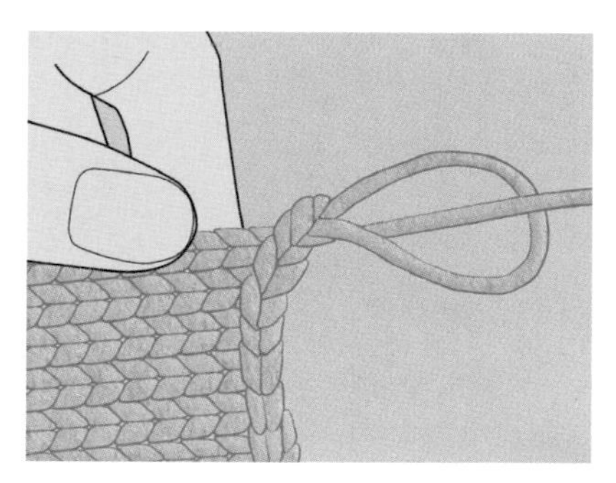

4 Repeat steps 2 and 3 until all stitches have been worked and 1 stitch remains on the right-hand needle. Make the last stitch loop larger, break the yarn, and draw through the loop to fasten off.

Knit and Purl

Most knitting is based on combinations of just two basic stitches— "knit" and "purl." Once you have mastered these stitches, you can work many different stitch patterns. The knit stitch is the simplest of all stitches. Knitting every row forms the ridged fabric called garter stitch. When you work a row of knit stitches alternated with a row of purl stitches this is referred to as stockinette stitch.

Knit

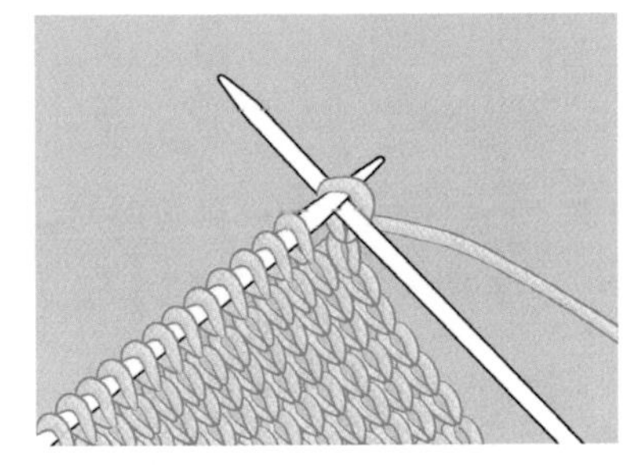

1 Hold the needle with the stitches to be knitted in your left hand with the yarn behind the work. Insert the right-hand needle into the first stitch on the needle from front to back.

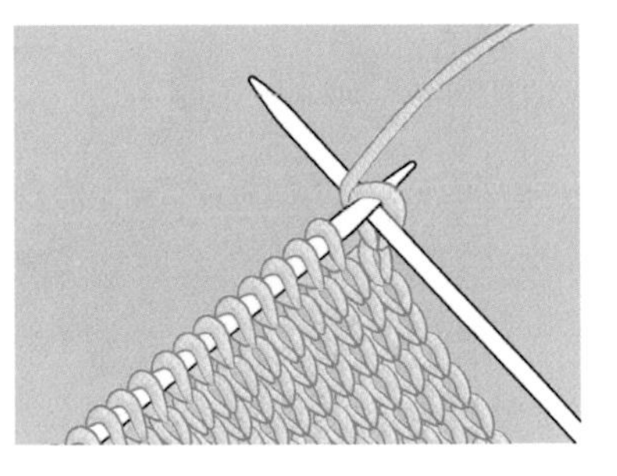

2 Take the yarn over the first stitch from back to front, forming a loop.

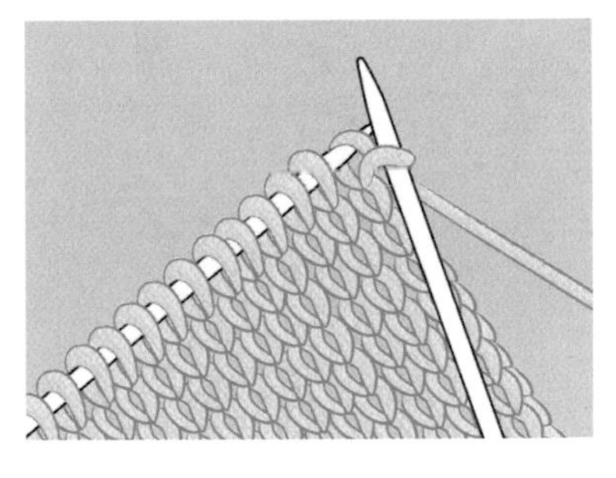

3 Bring the needle and the new loop to the front of the work through the stitch, and then slide the original stitch off the left-hand needle.

Purl

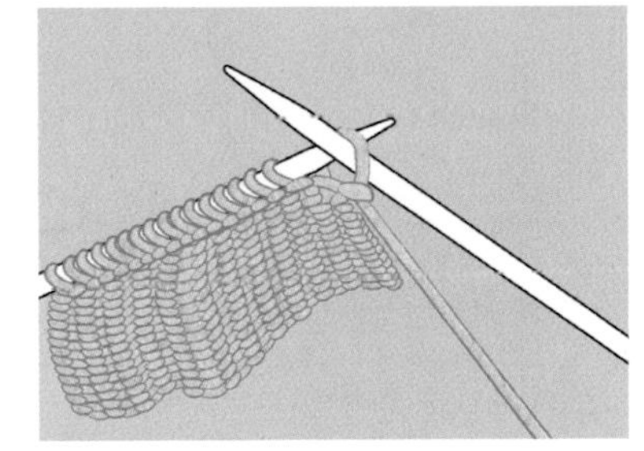

1 Hold the needle with the stitches to be purled in the left hand, with the yarn at the front of the work. Insert the right-hand needle through the front of the stitch, from right to left.

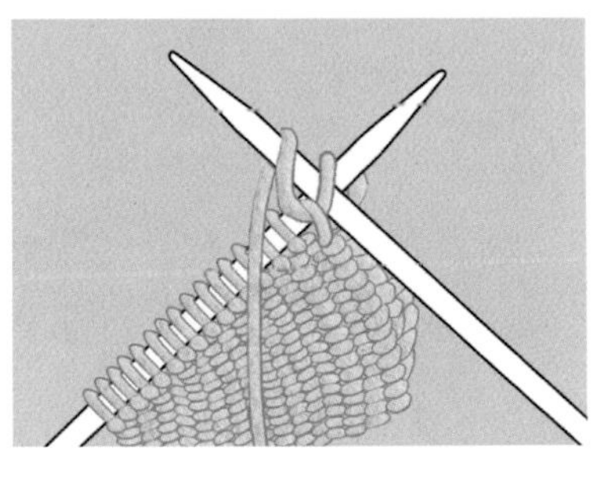

2 Take the yarn over and under the first stitch, forming a loop.

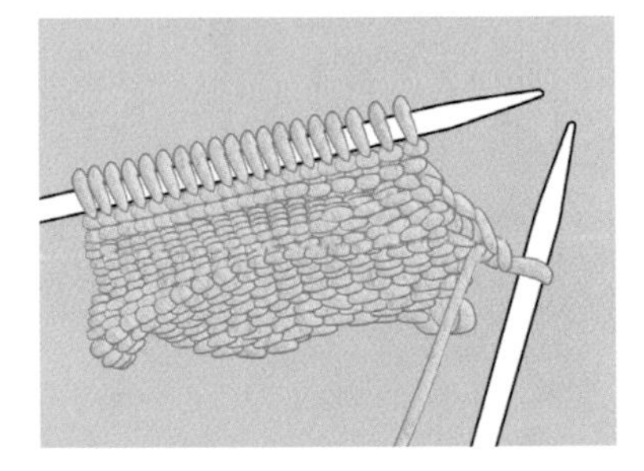

3 Take the needle and the new loop through the back and slide the original stitch off the left-hand needle.

Shaping Techniques—Increasing

Shaping techniques are used to create shapes in a piece of knitting. Increasing techniques are used to make the fabric wider by adding to the number of stitches. The two most common ways of increasing are Make 1 (M1), which creates an increase between two stitches, and increasing by knitting into the front and back of a stitch (k1f&b), which is best worked at the beginning or end of the knitted piece. Both increasing and decreasing techniques are usually worked at least one stitch in from the edge to make sewing up and picking up stitches easier.

M1—Make 1

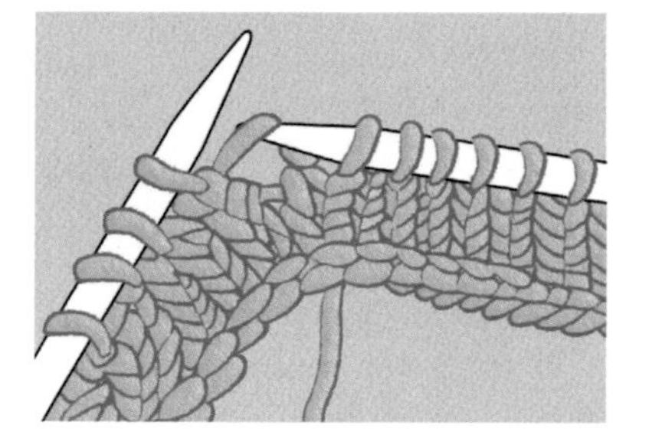

1 Insert the tip of the right-hand needle from front to back beneath the horizontal bar of yarn between 2 stitches where you want the increase.

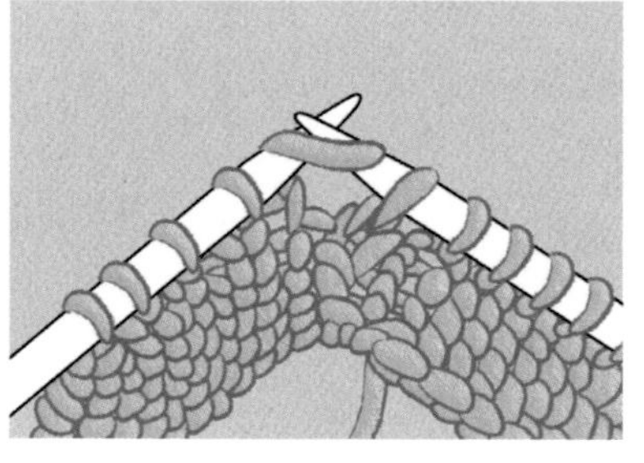

2 Slip the bar onto the left-hand needle.

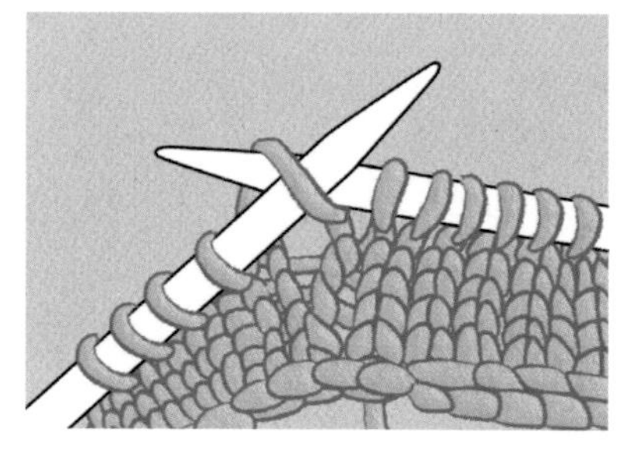

3 Create the new stitch by knitting through the back of the loop. This twists the loop and avoids making a hole.

k1f&b

This usually means knitting into the front and then the back of the same stitch. This increase is best worked at either the beginning or end of the knitted piece, as it is not very neat.

1 Work to where the extra stitch is needed. Knit into the front of the next stitch on the left knitting needle without slipping it off.

2 With the stitch still on the left needle and the yarn at the back, knit into the back of the same stitch and slip it from the needle.

Shaping Techniques—Decreasing

Decreasing techniques are used to make the fabric narrower by reducing the number of stitches. Various techniques are used, depending on whether the decrease needs to slope to the left or the right.

Sloping to the right

k2tog—knit 2 stitches together

To decrease a stitch knitwise, insert the needle from left to right through the first 2 stitches on the left-hand needle and knit as you would normally, slipping both stitches off the needle at the same time.

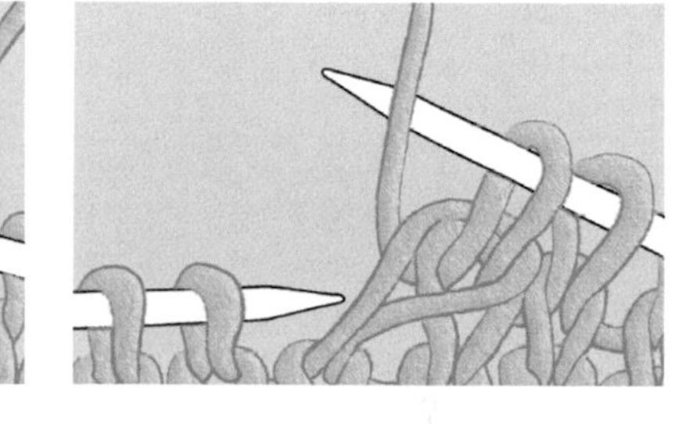

p2tog—purl 2 stitches together

To decrease a stitch purlwise, insert the needle from right to left through the first 2 stitches on the left-hand needle and purl as you would normally, slipping both stitches off the needle at the same time.

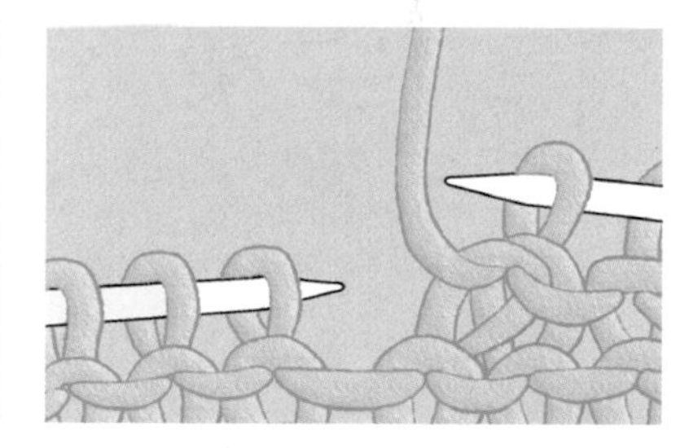

Sloping to the left

ssk—slip, slip, knit

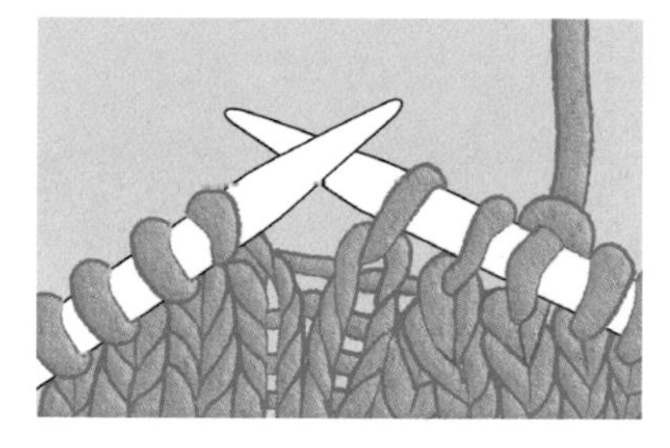

1 To decrease knitwise, slip 2 stitches knitwise one at a time from the left- to the right-hand needle.

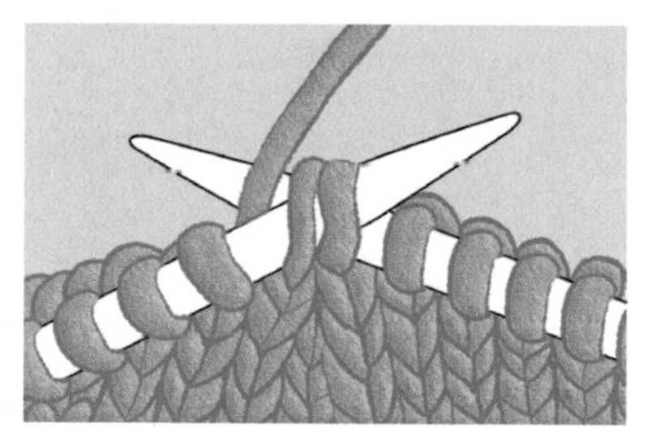

2 Insert the tip of the left-hand needle from left to right through the front loop of both stitches.

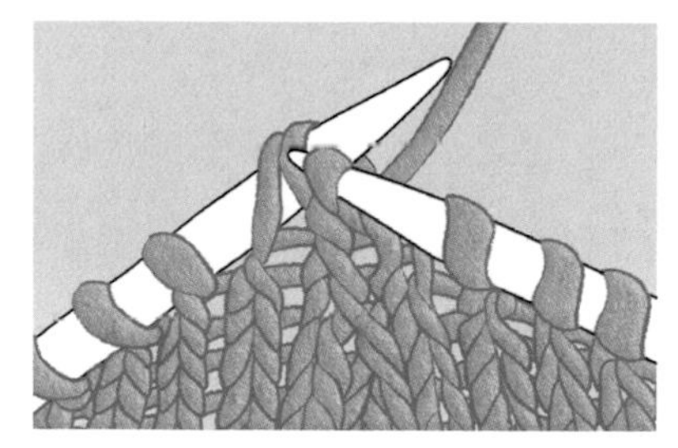

3 Knit them together.

skop—slip, knit, pass slipped stitch over

Slip the first stitch from the left-hand to the right-hand needle without working it. Knit the next stitch, then pass the slipped stitch over the worked stitch and off the needle.

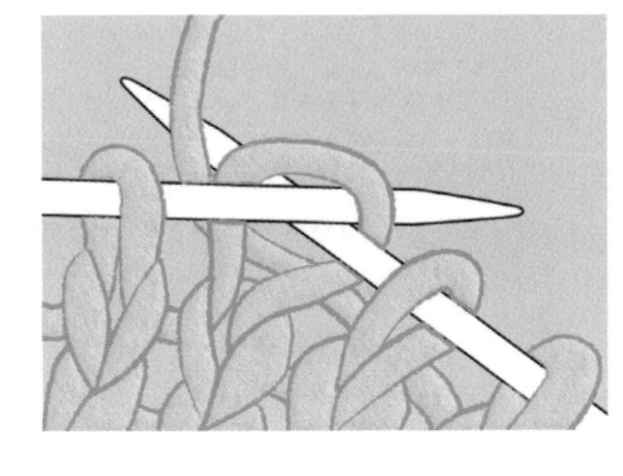

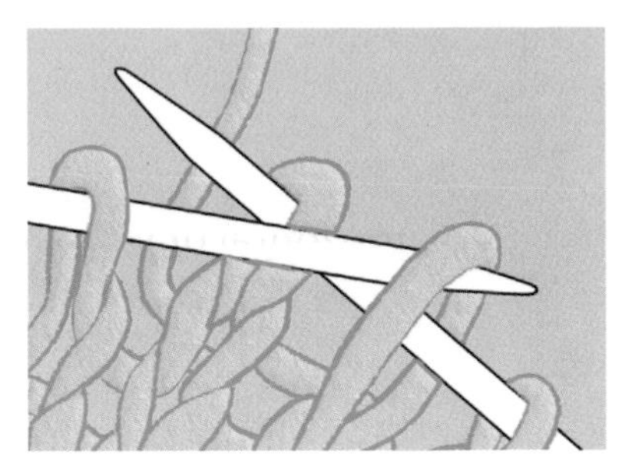

k2togtbl—knit 2 stitches together through back loop

To decrease a stitch knitwise, first insert the needle from right to left through the back loop of the first 2 stitches on the left-hand needle. Knit as normal, slipping both stitches off the needle at the same time.

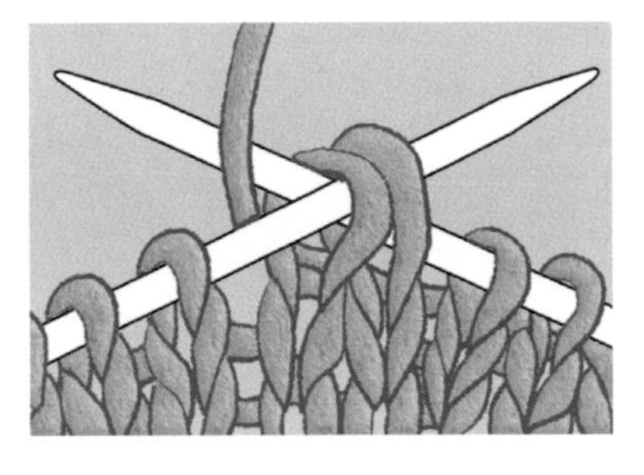

p2togtbl—purl 2 stitches together through the back loop

Insert the right-hand needle from left to right through the back loop of the first 2 stitches on the left needle. Purl as normal, slipping both stitches off the needle at the same time.

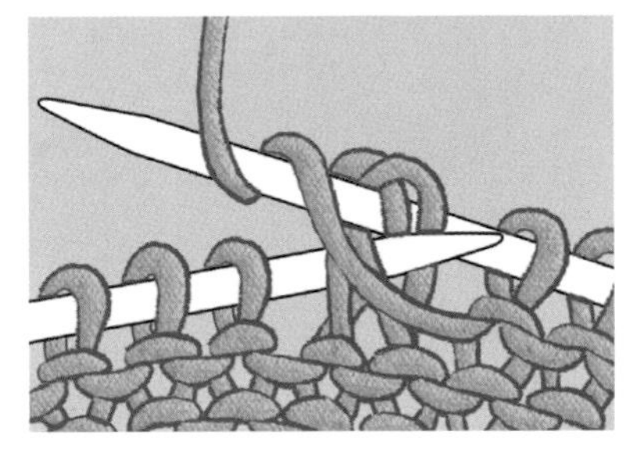

Picking Up Stitches

Some knitting patterns will ask you to pick up stitches along either a horizontal or vertical edge. Stitches must be picked up evenly along the required edge using a knitting needle and yarn to create the stitches you will then work into.

Horizontal edge

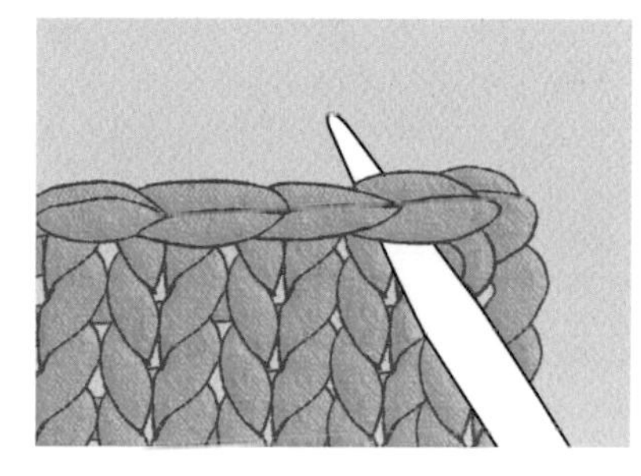

1 When picking up stitches along a bound-off or cast-on edge, work into 1 full stitch above or below to give a neater finish. Holding the needle in your right hand, insert the tip into the center of the first full stitch from front to back.

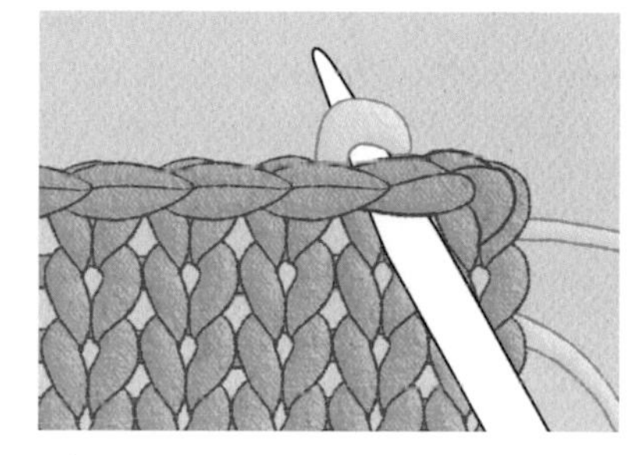

2 Wrap the yarn around the needle as if to work a knit stitch.

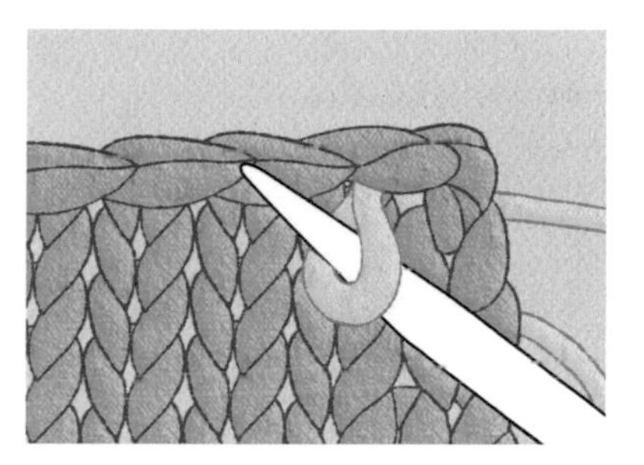

3 Pull the loop on the needle through to the front of the fabric to create a new stitch. Repeat these three steps until you have the required amount of stitches.

Vertical edge

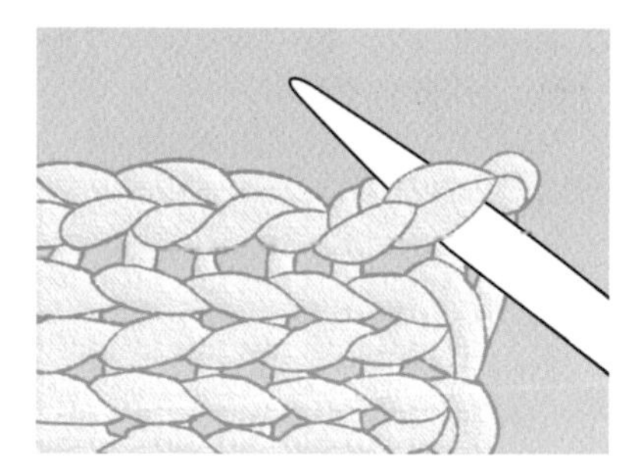

1 When picking up along an edge, work 1 full stitch in from the edge. Holding the needle in your right hand, insert the tip between the first and second stitches from the front to the back.

2 Wrap the yarn around the needle to work a knit stitch, and then pull the loop on the needle through to the front of the fabric to create a new stitch. Repeat these steps until you have the required amount of stitches.

Seams

Mattress stitch

A mattress stitch, sewn with a blunt tapestry needle, is the neatest and most discreet way to make a seam.

With right sides of both pieces of fabric toward you, secure yarn at the bottom of one piece. Pass needle to other section and pick up one stitch, which you can see on the needle in this picture. Pull yarn through and pull tightly. Insert needle through one stitch of first section, entering where the yarn exited previously. Continue in this way, from one side to the other as if lacing a corset, until you reach the last stitch. Secure tightly. If you have entered through the right section as shown opposite, the seam will be virtually indistinguishable from the rest of the fabric.

Always be sure to use the same color of yarn as in the main body of work (the contrasting yarn in the picture is just to highlight the technique) so that when the seams are pulled and moved when worn, the joining yarn cannot be seen. Some yarns may be too weak or fancy to sew along a seam, so double these up, add a stronger yarn to the original, or use a different yarn, but ensure it is the same color.

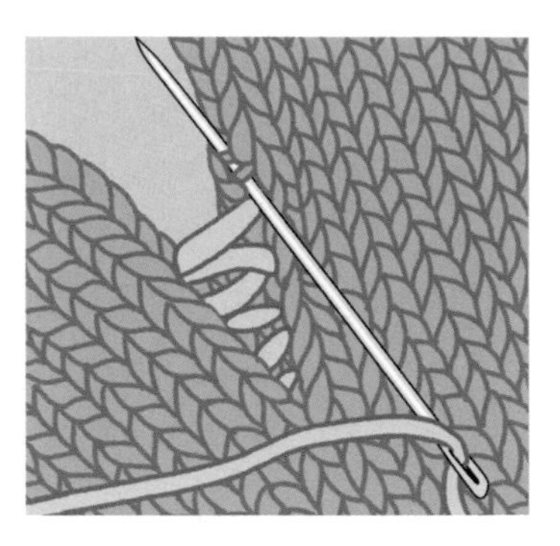

Grafting

Grafting the toe in a sock is the original use for this technique, but it is fabulous for many different seams. The shoulder seam worked in short rows lends itself well to grafting, but any two pieces of knitting that have been left on the needles rather than cast off can be grafted together using grafting or "Kitchener stitch" for an invisible seam.

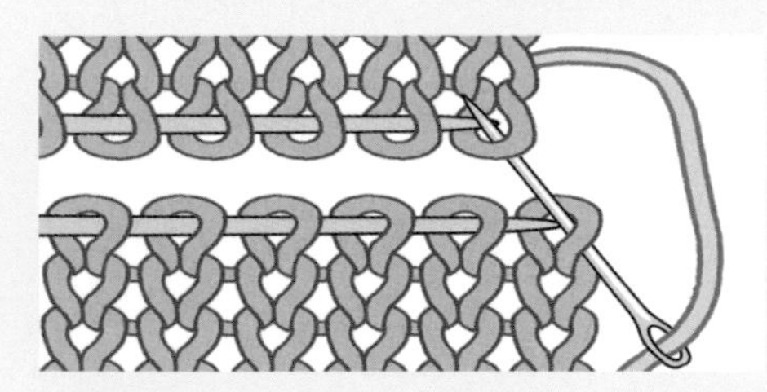

1 Using the knitting yarn, work from right to left. From the back of the fabric, bring the needle through the first knitted stitch of the lower fabric, and through the first stitch of the upper fabric.

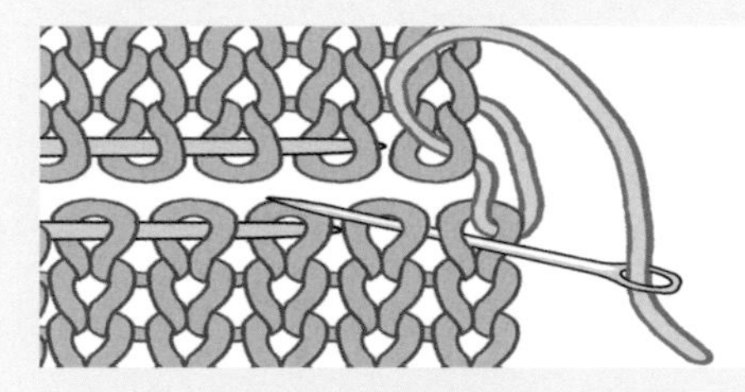

2 From the front, thread the needle back through the center of the first stitch on the lower fabric where the yarn leaves, then out of the center of the next stitch on the left.

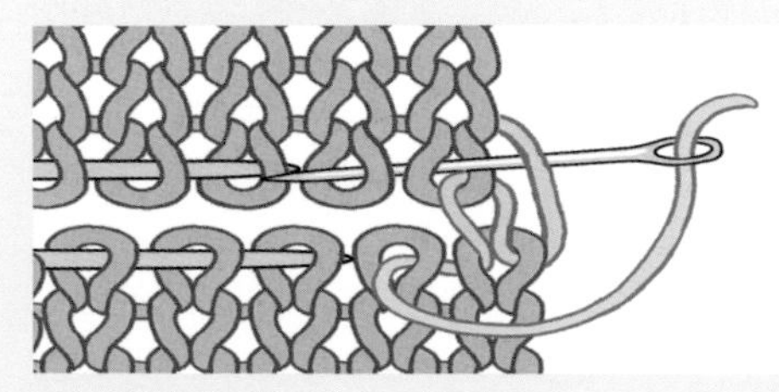

3 Thread the needle through the center of the top stitch and along the center of the next.

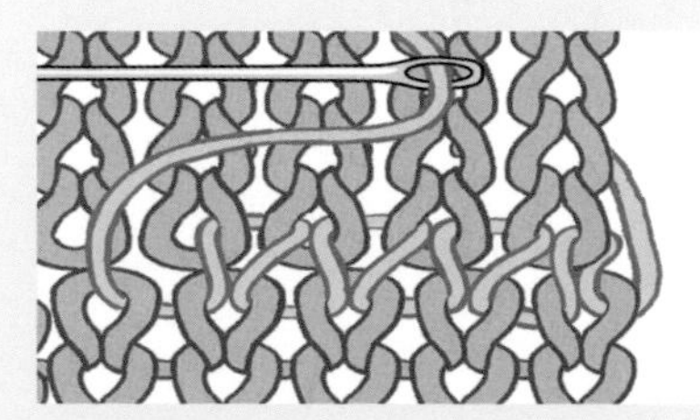

4 Continue like this and, as each stitch is worked, keep slipping the knitting needle from them.

Colorwork

Stranding or "Fair Isle" technique

Stranding is where a color that is not being used is carried across the back of the work, creating "floats" on the reverse of the fabric.

Stranding one-handed on knit rows or rounds

Stranding with one hand, if you knit the English way, involves dropping one yarn after use, then picking up another from underneath and carrying it across the back of the work. It is important not to twist the yarns in the changeover between the colors. When using the continental method of knitting, you place both colors on your index finger. The main color should always be closest to your knitting and the contrast next to it. Try to keep their position constant to avoid unnecessary twisting.

On a right-side (knit) row: Using the main color, work the desired number of stitches. Drop main color. Using your right hand, bring the second color from underneath, across the back of the work, over the top of the first yarn, and work the next stitches, being careful not to pull the yarn too tightly and to maintain an even tension.

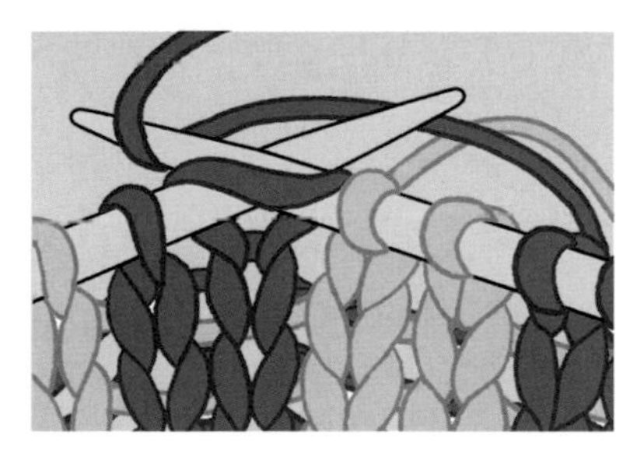

Stranding two-handed on a knit row or round

If you knit the English way, using the stranding technique with two hands is faster than using just one since the yarns do not need to be dropped between color changes. Hold one color over the forefinger of the left hand and the other according to the style in which you knit in the right hand.

When the stranded technique has been worked correctly, the carried yarn (floats) sits horizontally over stitches on the reverse side of the work.

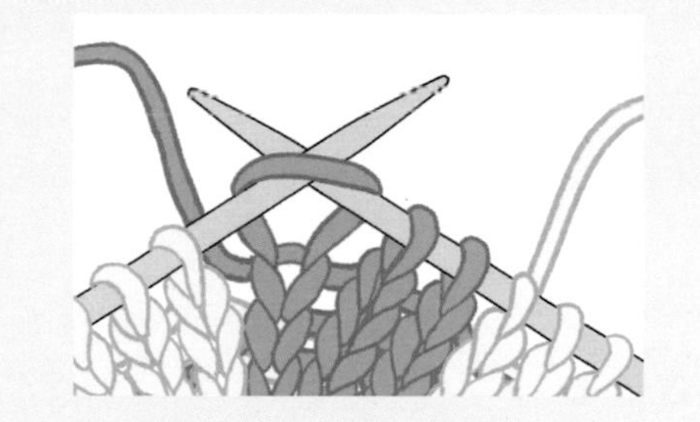

1 On a right-side (knit) row, using the main color and the continental method, work your stitches.

2 Using your right hand, bring the second color across the back of the work, over the top of the first yarn, and work the next stitches, being careful not to pull the yarn too tightly and to maintain an even tension.

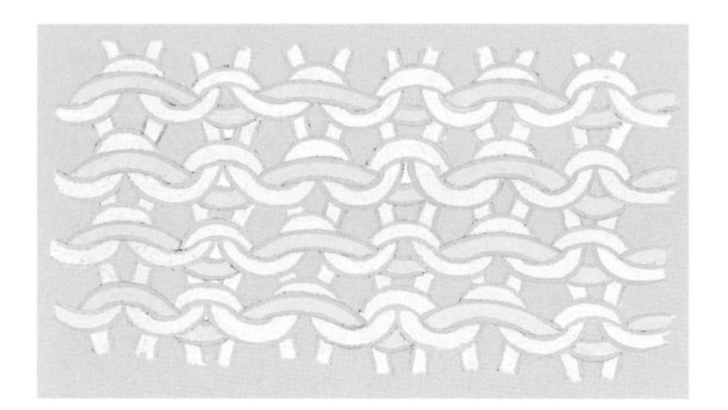

Weaving floats

If you are using the stranding technique, and the yarn is not going to be in use for more than 5 to 7 stitches, then weaving (or "catching") the floats is the best way of preventing them from hanging loose on the reverse of the fabric, where they can get caught or snagged when the piece is in use.

The yarn not in use is woven over and under, as in the illustration above, making a very firm fabric. Take care that the contrast color does not show through to the right side.

Intarsia

The intarsia method, which is the most widely used technique in this book, creates separate areas of color within the piece. A separate length of yarn is used for each section of colored knitting, and the yarns are twisted where they meet to create a single piece.

Intarsia is best worked over stockinette stitch, although areas of more textural stitching such as garter stitch and moss stitch can also look very effective when used in conjunction with intarsia.

Before you settle down to work, read through the pattern carefully and check how much yarn you need in each color. To work intarsia effectively you will need to learn a few basic techniques: Bobbin winding, joining in new colors, and changing from one color to another on both a knit and a purl row.

Bobbins

Bobbins are used when you do not wish to have a whole ball of yarn attached to the knitted piece while working intarsia. For larger areas of color you may wish to wrap the yarn in small plastic bags, secured with rubber bands to prevent tangling. You can buy plastic bobbins and wrap your yarn around them, or make your own.

1 Wrap the yarn around the thumb and finger of your right hand in the form of a figure eight.
2 Carefully remove the yarn from your fingers and cut it from the ball. Wind the loose end of yarn around the center of the figure eight and secure it tightly.

When using a bobbin, pull the yarn from the center a little at a time and keep it as close to the work as possible to avoid tangling.

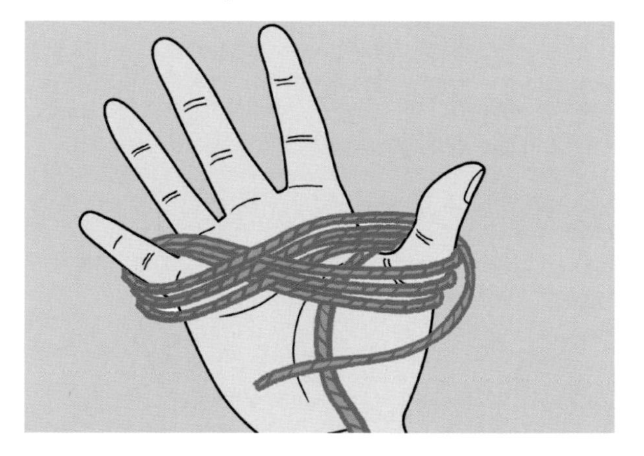

Joining in a new color

You may find that a new color of yarn is needed across a row of stitches, or that an existing bobbin is running out. In these cases you will need to join in a new color.

1 Insert the right-hand needle into the next stitch. Place the yarn over the working yarn and between the two needles, with the tail end to the left side.
2 Bring the new yarn up from under the existing yarn and knit, dropping both yarns from the left needle after you have done so.

Changing colors

When working an intarsia design, colored areas of fabric are worked from separate balls. If these areas are not joined together in some way, you will end up with individual pieces of color with large gaps in between. Simply cross the yarns to ensure that the knitting stays as one piece.

Changing color on a knit row: Work to the point where you need to change color. Insert the right-hand needle into the next stitch knitwise. Take the first color over the top of the second color and drop. Pick up the second color, ensuring that the yarns remain twisted, and continue according to the pattern.

Changing color on a purl row: Work to the point where you need to change color. Insert the right-hand needle into the next stitch purlwise. Take the first color over the top of the second color and drop. Pick up the second color, ensuring that the yarns remain twisted, and continue according to the pattern.

Reading a chart

All intarsia and most stranding patterns are set out in the form of a chart. Charts are read as for lace and cable charts from bottom to top, read from right to left on a RS row, and from left to right on a WS row (if you knit in rows). When knitting in the round, read charts from bottom to top, from right to left on each row.

Most patterns are now printed in color, but those printed in black and white will have a key to one side describing what colors are placed where, with each color represented by a symbol.

It is a good idea to photocopy the pattern, so that you can mark off rows as you work, or use a ruler to mark the row you are on. Photocopying is also useful if the chart is small, as you can enlarge it to a more readable size.

Reading chart symbols

Some charts in this book contain symbols for different stitches:

☐	K on RS, P on WS
●	Seed stitch
—	Garter
/	K2tog on RS, p2tog on WS
M	Make 1 (M1) knitwise on RS, M1 purlwise on WS
⌒	BO

Duplicate stitch

Duplicate stitch copies the structure and appearance of a knitted stitch.

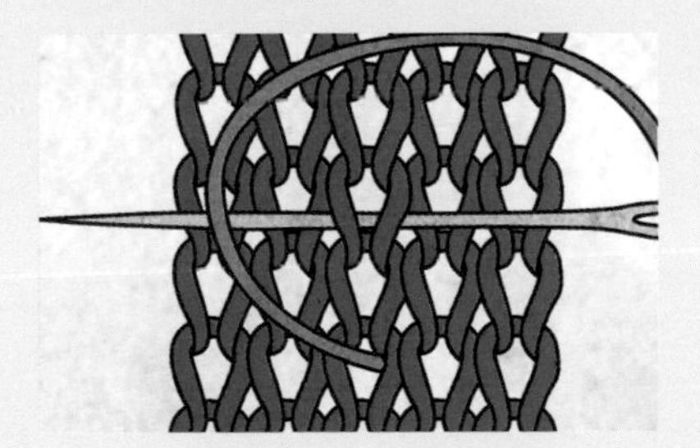

1 Bring the needle out at the base of the knitted stitch to be duplicated. Pass the needle behind the two "legs" of the stitch above and pull through.

2 Insert the needle again at the base of the same knitted stitch where it first emerged, and bring it out at the base of the next knitted stitch to be duplicated.

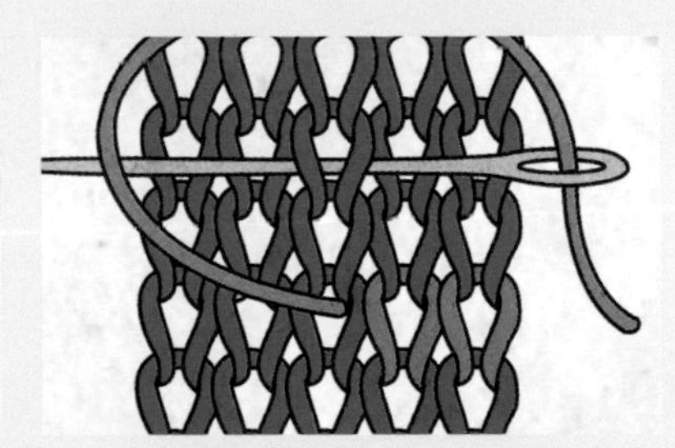

3 Repeat as needed.

1 Sans Serif

"Sans serif" means simply "without serif." A serif is a small tail at the end of the stroke of a letter. Sans serif (sometimes called "Grotesque" or "Gothic") is a large typeface group that includes the very popular fonts Tahoma, Arial, Verdana, and, of course, the typeface many consider to be the most beautiful sans serif ever designed, Helvetica.

Despite looking modern to the contemporary eye, sans serif typefaces have been used since as early as the fifth century BCE in Greek, Etruscan, and Latin inscriptions. Its modern usage in print dates to the eighteenth century's neoclassical movement, when all things Greek and Latin were revered. First used for impact in text (rather as we would use bold or italic), the application of sans serif migrated first to headers and finally to widespread acceptance as an in-text font. While serif fonts remain popular today on the printed page, sans serif now rules online, because of its clear readability and lack of distortion when converted to pixels.

In knitting, too, the sans serif font works best when clear readability is required. Knitting stitches are a bit like pixels, and consequently, letters that are rendered as knit stitches are most clear when serifs are not included. So the projects in this chapter, including the "STOP" Sign Doorstop (page 29) and the Felted Pencil Case (page 35), have bold, clear, unambiguous text, which marries well with the concept of the projects. Use the Sans Serif charts (pages 108–11) in your own projects when your message is bold and clear and the typeface needs to match.

Alphabet Pillow

As comfortable as it is educational, this alphabet pillow is the perfect way to test and show off your intarsia and stranding skills.

The pattern

Finished size: 24½ in/62 cm by 15¾ in/40 cm
Gauge: 27 sts and 34 rows over 4 in/10 cm in st st on US 2/3 mm needles
Note: Check your gauge—if fewer sts or rows, use smaller needles; if more, then use larger needles.

Letter motif

This project uses both upper- and lowercase Sans Serif alphabets featured on pages 108–11. The pillow charts on page 28 were designed so that the 1 st gap between each letter's upper- and lowercase form is arranged as a central column, with each uppercase letter aligned at the top. If using different letters, it is recommended that you arrange them in the same manner. If using words rather than letters, be sure to center them over the 168 st space (allowing at least 10 sts on either side). You may want to experiment with different spacings and alignments when charting out your own alphabets or words. ▶

You will need

Yarn

DMC Natura Just Cotton (super-fine weight, 4 ply, 100% cotton, approx. 170 yd/155 m per 1¾ oz/50 g)
[MC] Coral (shade N18), 1 ball
[CC] Ivory Cream (shade N02), 1 ball

Needles

US 2/3 mm knitting needles
Tapestry needle

Other

Scissors
Pillow form, at least 24½ in/62 cm by 15¾ in/40 cm or closest size available (can be cut to fit)

Aa Bb Cc D
Ee Ff Gg H
Ii Jj Kk L

Pillow front

Using MC, CO 168 sts.

Starting with a k row, work 24 rows in st st.

Commence Front Chart

With MC for the background and CC for the letters, work rows 1–87 of the Front Chart (page 28) using the stranding technique.

Cont in MC only, work 25 rows in st st.

BO.

Pillow back

Using MC, CO 168 sts.

Starting with a k row, work 10 rows in st st.

Commence Back Chart

With MC for the background and CC for the letters, work rows 1–116 of the Back Chart (page 28) using the stranding technique.

Cont in MC only, work 10 rows in st st.

BO.

Finishing

Weave in all ends neatly and block or press the pieces according to the instructions on the ball band. Sew back and front pieces together around the side and top edges. Insert the pillow form. If the pillow form is too big, undo one seam of its lining and remove the filling. Measure the lining and cut to fit the knitted pillow. Sew back together, leaving a gap for the stuffing. Refill with stuffing and sew gap closed. Sew rem base seam of the cover closed. ▶

Alphabet Pillow: Front Chart

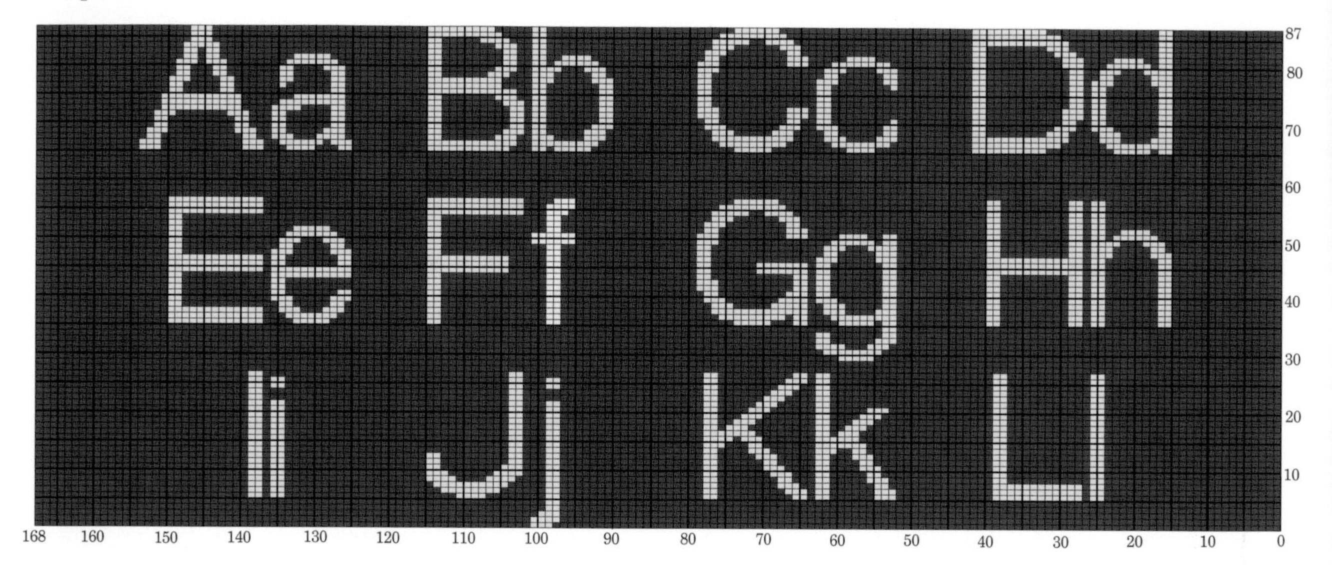

Alphabet Pillow: Back Chart

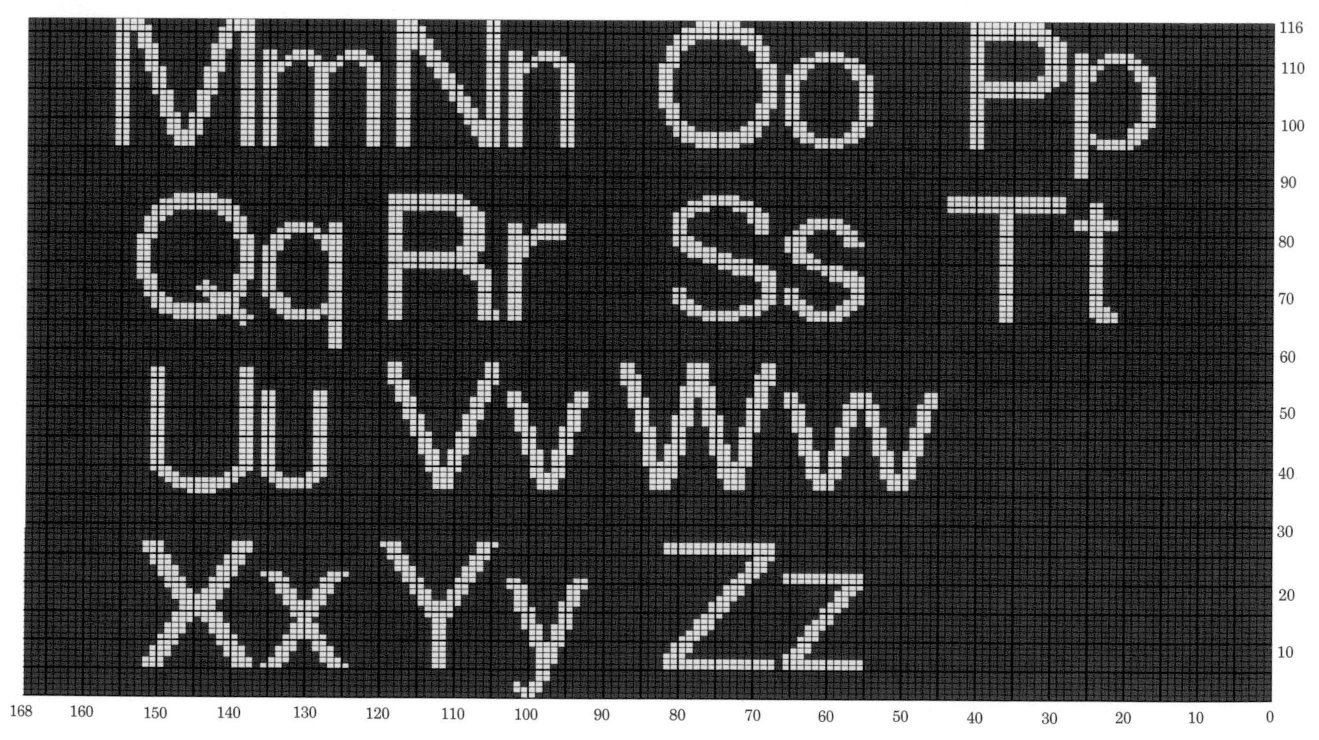

"STOP" Sign Doorstop

Designed to mimic a stop sign, this functional piece makes a bold statement using the sans serif font. Using dried beans as stuffing provides stability and weight and ensures that doors will do exactly as the sign says.

The pattern

Finished size: 12 in/30 cm by 15 in/38 cm
Gauge: 26 sts and 32 rows over 4 in/10 cm in st st on US 3/3.25 mm knitting needles

Letter motif

Use the "STOP" Sign Doorstop Chart on page 31. If you are changing the wording, use the Sans Serif Uppercase Charts on pages 108–9. You will be able to fit a maximum of 4 letters onto the doorstop depending on your chosen letters. Your chosen combination of letters plus 2 sts between each letter should not exceed 65 sts. If using fewer than 65 sts, be sure to center your letters within the total 73 st space at the point in the pattern where the chart commences.

Front

** Using MC, CO 33 sts.
Row 1 (RS): Knit.
Row 2 (WS): Purl.
Row 3: K1, M1, k to last st, M1, k1. *2 sts inc.*
Row 4: Purl.
Rep rows 3 and 4 until you have 73 sts.

Work 10 rows in st st without inc, ending with a p row.

Commence "STOP" Sign Doorstop Chart

Work rows 1–23 of chart using the stranding technique. ▶

You will need

Yarn

Rowan Pure Wool DK (100% wool, approx. 136 yd/124 m per 1¾ oz/50 g)
[MC] Red (shade 36), 3 balls
[CC] White (shade 12), 1 ball

Needles

US 3/3.25 mm knitting needles
Tapestry needle

Other

Scissors
2 pieces of sturdy cardstock, at least 12 in/30 cm by 15 in/38 cm
Dried beans, 17 oz/500 g
Polyester toy stuffing

STOP

After chart, cont with MC only and work 10 rows in st st without inc.

Commence dec as follows:
Row 1: K1, ssk, k to last 3 sts, k2tog, k1. *2 sts dec.*
Row 2: Purl.
Rep last 2 rows until 33 sts rem.

BO all sts.

Back

Work as for front from ** until you have 73 sts.

Work 43 rows in st st, ending with a p row.

Commence dec as follows:
Row 1 (RS): K1, ssk, k to last 3 sts, k2tog, k1. *2 sts dec.*
Row 2 (WS): Purl.
Rep last 2 rows until 33 sts remain.
BO all sts on RS. Weave in ends.

Gusset

Using CC, CO 14 sts.

Starting with a k row, work in st st until piece measures 17¾ in/45 cm (or length required to fit around back piece when slightly stretched), ending with a p row.

BO all sts on RS. Weave in ends.

Finishing

Weave in ends and press or block pieces according to the ball band instructions. Using mattress stitch, attach the gusset around the entire back seam. Sew the bottom half of the front to gusset.

Cut two octagons from cardstock, slightly larger than front and back pieces to ensure a slight stretch. Insert these into the pillow and pour dried beans into the pillow between them. Cont seaming around top of piece, now filling with toy stuffing as you go. Finish seam and close short side of gusset.

"STOP" Sign Doorstop Chart

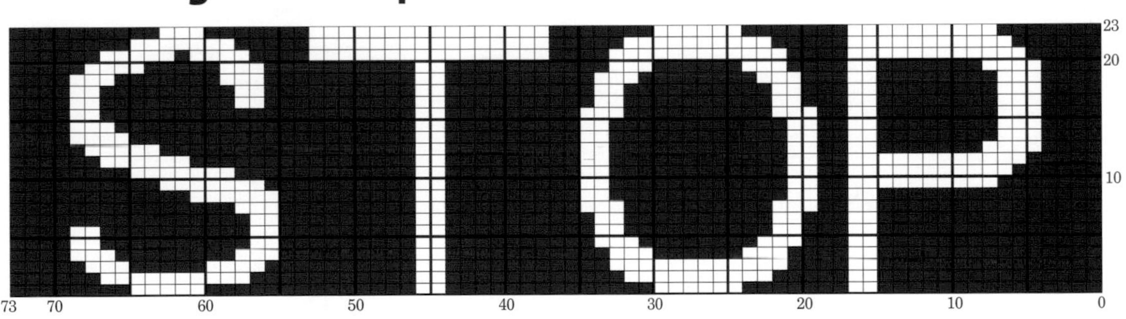

Letter Tile Coasters

These letter tile coasters are ideal for spelling out a statement of intent to your dinner guests (i.e. "it's 'vino' time"), but the pattern can easily be adapted to other uses such as creating colorful lettered bunting for a special occasion.

The pattern

Finished size: 3¼ in/8.25 cm square
Gauge: 27 sts and 34 rows over 4 in/10 cm measured over st st on US 2/3 mm needles

Letter motif

This project uses the "VINO" Letter Tile Charts on page 34, or for different letters, the Sans Serif Uppercase Charts featured on pages 108–9. On the chart of your chosen letter, draw a box around the letter that is 23 sts wide and 22 rows high, making sure the letter is in the center. If your letter has an even number of sts, one side will have 1 st extra.

Coasters

Using MC, CO 17 sts.

Row 1 (RS): Knit.
Row 2 (WS): P1f&b, p to last st, p1f&b. *19 sts*
Row 3: K1f&b, k to last st, k1f&b. *21 sts*
Row 4: As row 2. *23 sts*

Commence "VINO" Letter Tile Chart

With MC for the background and CC for the letter, cont in st st and work rows 1–22 of the chart using the stranding technique.

Cont in MC only as follows:
Row 27: Knit.
Row 28: P2tog, p to last st, p2tog. *21 sts*
Row 29: K2tog, k to last st, k2tog. *19 sts*
Row 30: As row 2. *17 sts.*

BO. ▶

You will need

Yarn

DMC Natura Just Cotton (4 ply, 100% cotton, approx. 170 yd/155 m per 1¾ oz/50 g)
[MC] Gardenia (shade N36), 1 ball
[CC] Noir (shade N11), 1 ball

Needles

US 2/3 mm knitting needles
Tapestry needle

Other

Scissors
Felt, 3¼ in/8.25 cm square, to back each coaster
Sewing needle and thread

Finishing

Weave in ends and block or press the coaster according to the instructions on the ball band.

Sew in all ends neatly. Using sewing thread, sl st the knitted coaster to the felt around all edges.

"VINO" Letter Tile Charts

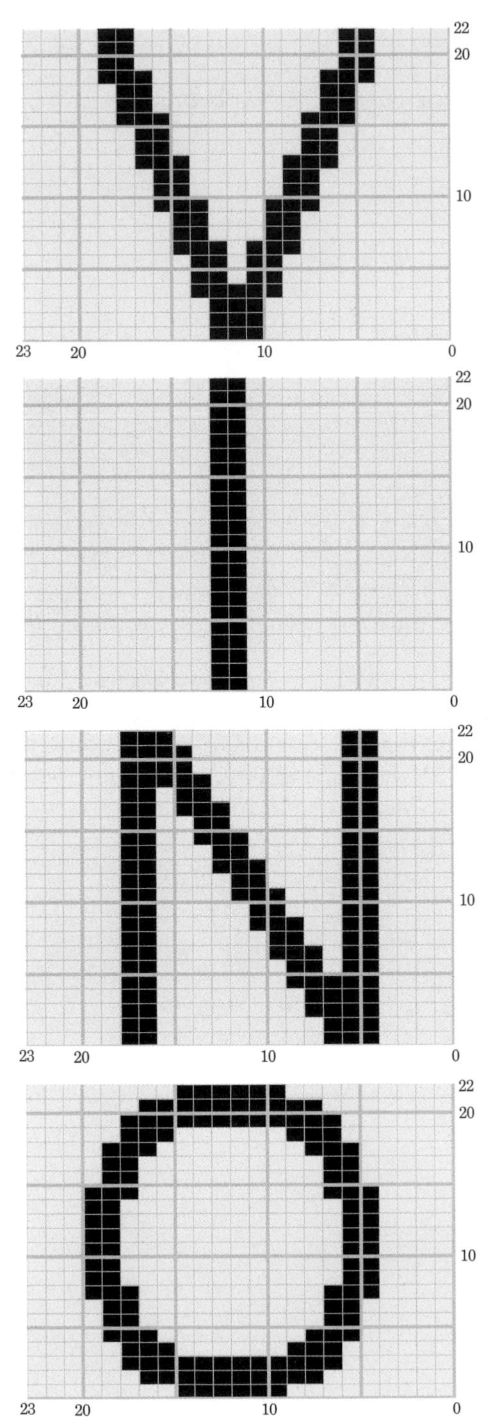

Felted Pencil Case

This fun and colorful project demonstrates what can be achieved with a few letters, some simple colorwork, and a little imagination. Take a mental trip to the Big Apple every time you reach for a pencil.

The pattern

Finished size: after felting, 8 in/20 cm by 5½ in/14 cm
Gauge: 20 sts and 26 rows over 4 in/10 cm in st st on US 7/4.5 mm needles before felting

Letter motif

This project uses the Checks and "Taxi" Charts on page 37. If you are changing the wording, use the Sans Serif Uppercase Charts on pages 108–9. You will be able to fit a maximum of 4 to 5 sans serif letters onto the pencil case depending on the chosen letters. Draw a box 1 square wider than your chosen letters. This will show you the amount of space you have between each letter. Make sure the placement of the word is centered before you start knitting.

Front panel

Using MC, CO 51 sts.

Starting with a k row, work 8 rows in st st.

Commence Checks Chart

Work rows 1–11 of Checks Chart using the stranding technique.

Using MC only, work 3 rows in st st.

Commence "Taxi" Chart

Work rows 1–21 of "Taxi" Chart using the intarsia technique.

Using MC only, work 5 rows in st st. ▶

You will need

Yarn

Rowan Creative Focus Worsted (75% wool/ 25% alpaca, 218 yd/200 m per 3½ oz/100 g)
[MC] Saffron (shade 03810), 1 ball
[CC1] Ebony (shade 00500), 1 ball
[CC2] Natural (shade 00100), 1 ball

Needles

US 7/4.5 mm knitting needles
Tapestry needle

Other

Scissors
Yellow closed-end zipper, 10 in/25 cm (trim the zipper to fit the width of your finished, felted pencil case, which may vary)
Sewing needle and thread to match zipper

taxi
GOLD-CAT

BO.

Back panel

Using MC pick up and k 51 sts along the cast-on edge of front panel.

Starting with a p row, work 7 rows in st st.

Commence Checks Chart

Work rows 1–11 of Checks Chart using the stranding technique.

Using MC only, work 29 rows in st st.

BO in k.

Finishing

Sew up the side seams using mattress stitch or back stitch and leave the top open. Stitch along the top opening with a cotton-based yarn or thread with running stitch. Felt the pencil case by hand or in a washing machine until the fabric is the finished size.

Leave to dry, then stitch zipper into top opening.

"Taxi" Chart

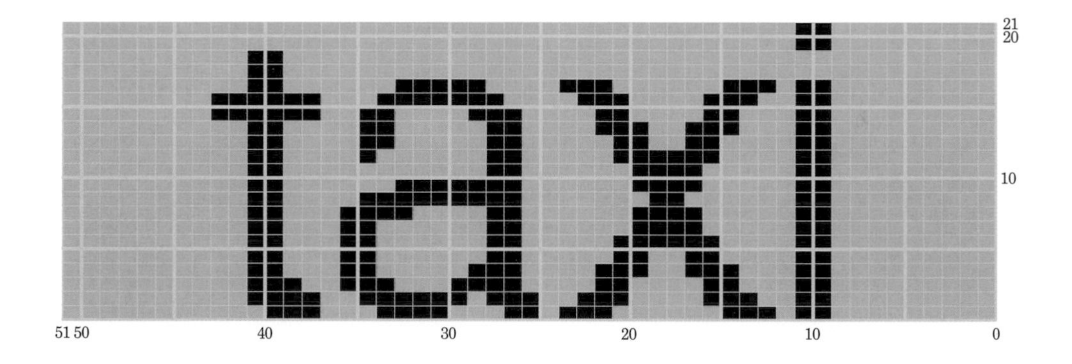

Checks Chart

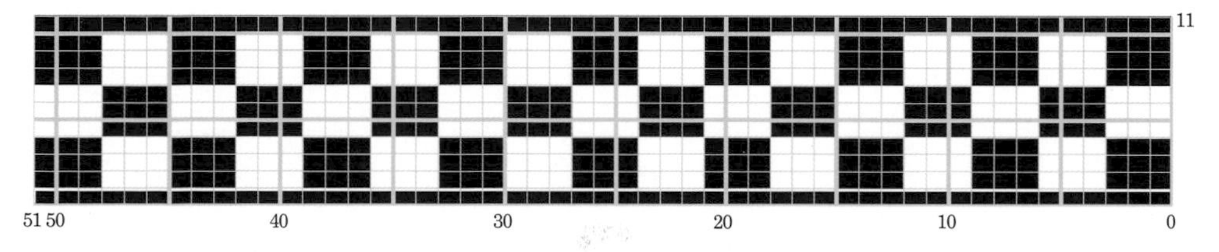

"Ciao" Mittens

Not only will these attractive mittens keep your hands warm all winter, but they also allow you to wave a message to your friends from the palms of your hands.

The pattern

Finished size: approx. 8 in/20 cm wide at cuff and 11½ in/29 cm long
Gauge: approx. 26 sts and 36 rows over 4 in/10 cm in st st on US 3/3.25 mm needles
Note: Sections of the pattern are specific to either the right or the left mitten. Ensure that you are working the correct part and have both a right and a left mitten.

Letter motif

Use the "Ciao" Chart on page 41. If you are changing the wording, use the Sans Serif Lowercase Charts featured on pages 110–11. You will be able to fit a maximum of 3 or 4 letters depending on your choice of letters. On the chart of each letter, draw a box around it that is 23 sts wide and allows 1 row above and below the letter. Three of the letters used in this design ("c," "a," and "o") are 17 rows tall, and the other, "i," is 21 rows tall ("j" is the tallest letter in the Sans Serif Lowercase Charts at 26 rows).

Each letter is given its own colored background that matches the length of the graph that is drawn around it; if you are using alternative letters, the stripe heights may vary. Place the charts vertically in sequence to make one large chart—remember you will be working from the bottom up. ▶

You will need

Yarn

Rowan Fine Tweed (4 ply, 100% wool, approx. 98 yd/90 m per 1 oz/25 g)
[MC] Bainbridge (shade 369), 1 ball
[CC1] Dent (shade 373), 1 ball
[CC2] Leyburn (shade 383), 1 ball
[CC3] Richmond (shade 381), 1 ball
[CC4] Nidd (shade 382), 1 ball
[CC5] Arncliffe (shade 360), 1 ball

Needles

US 3/3.25 mm knitting needles
US 2/3 mm knitting needles

Other

Scissors

Cuff

Using smaller needles and MC, CO 50 sts.

Row 1 (RS): K2, * p1, k2; rep from * to end.
Row 2 (WS): P2, * k2, p2; rep from * to end.
Rep prev 2 rows a further 8 times.

Right mitten only

Commence "Ciao" Chart

Next row (RS): Change to larger needles and using CC1, k27, k row 1 of chart using the intarsia technique and CC5 for the letter sts.
Next row (WS): P foll row 2 of chart.

Cont working as set to row 19.

Change to CC2 and, keeping CC5 for the lettering, work rows 20–22 of chart.

Place thumb

Maintaining colors, cont in patt as set from chart and commence thumb gusset inc as follows:

Row 23 (RS): K26, m1, k to end. *51 sts*
Rows 24–26: Work in st st from chart as set.
Row 27: K26, m1, k1, m1, k to end. *53 sts*
Row 28 and every foll WS row: Purl.
Row 29: K26, m1, k3, m1, k to end. *55 sts*
Row 31: K26, m1, k5, m1, k to end. *57 sts*
Row 33: K26, m1, k7, m1, k to end. *59 sts*
Row 35: K26, m1, k9, m1, k to end. *61 sts*
Row 37: K26, m1, k11, m1, k to end. *63 sts*
Change to CC3 and keep working patt from chart as set.
Row 39: Change to yarn CC4 and cont working in patt from chart as set; k26, m1, k13, m1, k to end. *65 sts*
Row 41: K26, m1, k15, m1, k to end. *67 sts*
Row 42: Purl.

Split thumb

Next row: K43, turn.
**** Next row (WS):** P17. You will now cont on these 17 sts, leaving rem sts on the needle.

Work 8 rows in st st.
If you want a longer thumb, add extra rows here.

Next row: K5, k2tog, k3, k2tog, k5. *15 sts*
Work 3 rows in st st.
Next row: K4, k2tog, k3, k2tog, k4. *13 sts*
Next row: K3, k2tog, k3, k2tog, k3. *11 sts*

Break yarn, leaving a 6 in/15 cm tail, thread through rem thumb sts, pull tight, and sew side seam of thumb.

Rejoin yarn to main mitten sts by picking up 2 sts at base of thumb and p to end of row. *51 sts*

Next row: K to the picked-up sts, k2tog, k to end of row, maintaining patt as set. *50 sts*

Cont working from chart as set and change colors as indicated through to end of row 78.

Shape top

Cont in patt and *at the same time* work dec on the foll rows:
Row 71: K1, * k2tog, k20, k2togtbl; rep from *, k1. *46 sts*
Row 75: K1, * k2tog, k18, k2togtbl; rep from *, k1. *42 sts*
Row 77: K1, * k2tog, k16, k2togtbl; rep from *, k1. *38 sts*
Row 79: K1, * k2tog, k14, k2togtbl; rep from *, k1. *34 sts*
Row 83: K1, * k2tog, k12, k2togtbl; rep from *, k1. *30 sts*
Row 85: K1, * k2tog, k10, k2togtbl; rep from *, k1. *26 sts*
Work one more WS row.

BO.

Left mitten only

Commence "Ciao" Chart

Work as for right mitten from cuff to end of row 22.

Place thumb

Maintaining colors, cont in patt as set from chart and commence thumb gusset inc as follows:
Row 23 (RS): K24, m1, k to end. *51 sts*
Rows 24–26: Work in st st from chart as set.
Row 27: K24, m1, k1, m1, k to end. *53 sts*

Row 28 and every foll WS row: Purl.
Row 29: K24, m1, k3, m1, k to end. *55 sts*
Row 31: K24, m1, k5, m1, k to end. *57 sts*
Row 33: K24, m1, k7, m1, k to end. *59 sts*
Row 35: K24, m1, k9, m1, k to end. *61 sts*
Row 37: K24, m1, k11, m1, k to end. *63 sts*
Row 39: Change to yarn CC4 and cont working in patt from chart as set; k24, m1, k13, m1, k to end. *65 sts*
Row 41: K24, m1, k15, m1, k to end. *67 sts*
Row 42: Purl.

Split thumb

Next row: K41, turn.

Now work as set for right mitten from ** to end.

Finishing

Weave in ends and join side seam. Block or press according to ball band instructions.

"Ciao" Chart

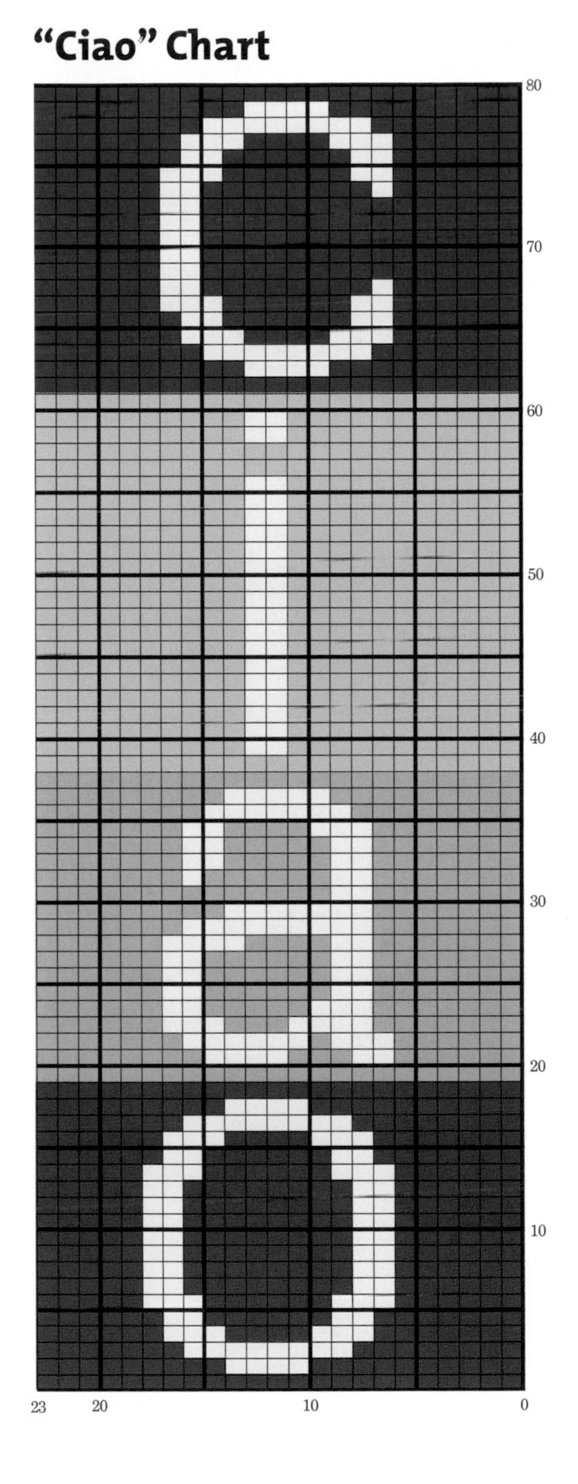

2 Serif

A serif is a small tail, flourish, or nonstructural detail at the end of the stroke (line) of a letter. The origin of the serif is not definitively known, but theories range from stonecutters in antiquity copying letters that had originally been made with brushstrokes, to those same stonecutters using serifs either to catch the light, to strengthen the carving, or to provide readability or clearer distinction between letters from far below. Serif typefaces are also sometimes called "Roman" due to their origins, and most users of Microsoft Word will be familiar with Times New Roman, one of the most widely used typefaces in the world, due to its popularity in word processing programs and printed books. The serif typeface group also includes such popular fonts as Georgia, Garamond, Baskerville, and Century.

When relatively modern printers started designing serif fonts in the fifteenth century, they used serifs for aesthetic reasons rather than structural ones. To our modern eye, sans serif fonts look clearer and more legible, but in the early days of printing, serif fonts were considered the most readable fonts. These serif fonts grew more popular than the once standard Gothic, or black letter (discussed in chapter 7) during the seventeenth century, because they were more readable, economical with space, and easy to print.

Serif fonts are still widely used today; some studies have found them to have greater readability in print than sans serif fonts, but there is no firm consensus on whether this is the case. Many people prefer serif fonts simply because of their familiarity. Printed books may look "odd" in sans serif because we are accustomed to serif fonts being used in print (this is most true in North America; in Europe, sans serif for print is becoming increasingly popular). Serif fonts work best in knitted projects where the knitter needs a warmly traditional, attractive, but still readable font, such as in the "Domus dulcis Domus" Wall Art (facing page) and the Bookstore Tote (page 47).

"Domus dulcis Domus" Wall Art

Spelling out "Home sweet Home" with a Latin twist, this wall art demonstrates the visual clarity that can be achieved with knitted typography. Adapt and expand this basic design to spell out any message you choose.

The pattern

Finished size: 10 in/25 cm square
Gauge: 27 sts and 34 rows over 4 in/10 in st st on US 3/3.25 mm needles
Note: Check your gauge—if fewer sts or rows, use smaller needles; if more, use larger needles.

Letter motif

Use the Wall Art Chart on page 45. If you are changing the wording, use the Serif Charts on pages 112–15. Your combined letters (a maximum of 5 or 6 letters) should not exceed 60 sts per line, with 1 st gaps between each letter, and a maximum of 3 lines. Ensure that your chosen letters are centered horizontally across the full 69 st space and vertically over 86 rows. For example, if using the phrase "Home sweet Home" instead, the total number of sts for "Home" including spaces is 52, so you would k8, work the letters and spaces, k9. The total number of sts for "sweet" is 54, so you would k7, work the letters and spaces, k8. (Both of these words have an even number of sts, so there will be 1 st more on one side of these words since the total number of sts for the Wall Art is odd.)

Wall Art

Using MC, CO 69 sts. ▶

You will need

Yarn

DMC Natura Just Cotton (4 ply, 100% cotton, approx. 170 yd/155 m per 1¾ oz/50 g)
[MC] Star Light (shade N27), 1 ball
[CC] Gardenia (shade N36), 1 ball

Needles

US 3/3.25 mm knitting needles

Other

Scissors
Frame to fit over the 10 in/25 cm square finished knitted sampler
Thin pressed mat board to fit frame
Double-sided adhesive tape

Domus
dulcis
Domus

Commence Wall Art Chart

With MC for the background and CC for the writing, work rows 1–86 of the chart below using the stranding and intarsia techniques.

BO.

Finishing

Weave in ends and block or press the wall art according to the instructions on the ball band. Place the wall art in the center of the mat board and put the frame over it to ensure the sampler is centered and the edges of the knitting are covered by the frame. Mark the wall art's position on the board and remove. Apply strips of double-sided tape around the board and peel off the backing tape. Making sure the words are straight, press the wall art down firmly so that the knitting is stuck to the board, and assemble the frame.

Wall Art Chart

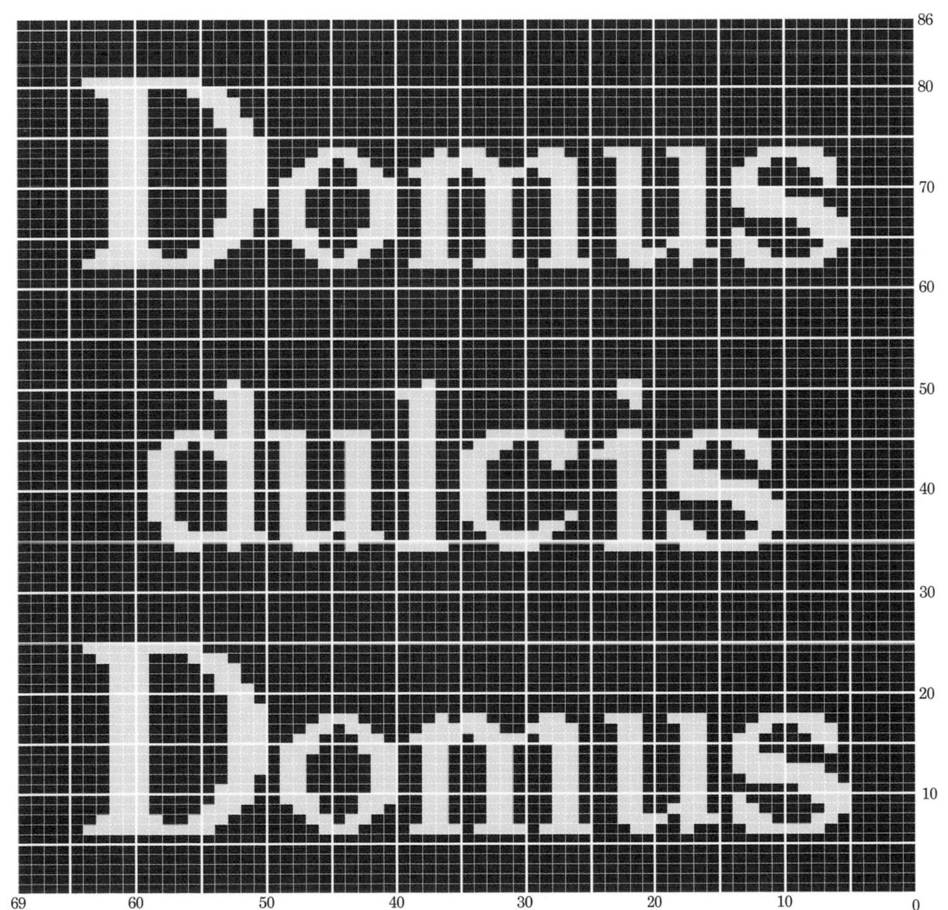

Dante
Books

Bookstore Tote

This tote bag is guaranteed to stand out from any others on the street. The serif font gives the bag a classic look that can be customized with the name of your favorite bookstore (real or imagined) or any other text that you want to show off along with your purchases.

The pattern

Finished Size: 12½ in/31.75 cm by 14 in/35.5 cm
Gauge: 22 sts and 28 rows over 4 in/10 cm in st st on US 6/4 mm needles

Letter motif

Use the Bookstore Tote Chart on page 48. If changing the wording, use the Serif Charts on pages 112–15. You will be able to fit a maximum of 5 letters into the box border per line (maximum 2 lines) depending on your chosen letters. Your chosen letters plus 1 st spaces between each letter should not exceed 54 sts. It is recommended that you center your words horizontally over the 58 st space within the box, and vertically over 46 rows, allowing 4 rows between lines.

Front

Using MC, CO 78 sts.

Starting with a k row, work in st st until piece measures 6 in/15 cm, ending with a p row.

Commence Bookstore Tote Chart

Using MC for the background and CC for the writing, and using stranding and intarsia techniques, work rows 1–50 of chart in st st.

Cont working in MC only working st st until piece measures 14 in/35.5 cm, ending with a k row. ▶

You will need

Yarn

Rowan Denim (DK, 100% cotton, 109 yd/100 m per 1¾ oz/50 g)
Rowan Cotton Glacé (DK, 100% cotton, 125 yd/115 m per ¾ oz/50 g)
[MC] Rowan Denim: Ecru (shade 324), 4 balls
[CC] Rowan Cotton Glacé: Poppy (shade 741), 1 ball

Needles

US 6/4 mm knitting needles
Tapestry needle

Other

Scissors
2 stitch markers
Lining fabric, 28¾ in/73 cm by 17 in/43 cm
Wide cotton tape or webbing for handles, 1 in/2.5 cm by 30 in/76 cm
Sewing needle and thread

Front Facing

**** Next row (WS) (foldline):** Knit.

Starting with a k row, work 8 rows in st st.

BO.

Back

Using MC, CO 78 sts.

Starting with a k row, work in st st until back measures same as front to foldline, ending with a k row.

Back Facing

Work back facing as given for front facing from **.

Finishing

Weave in ends and block or press pieces according to the instructions on the ball band. Sew back and front tog around side edges and base. Fold facing to WS and sl st into place. Measure finished width of bag and finished length from base to lower edge of facing. Cut two pieces of lining fabric to these measurements, adding ⅝ in/1.5 cm seam allowance to all edges. Sew the two pieces of lining tog around side and base edges. Fold seam allowance to WS along top edge and press. Make two handles by cutting the 30 in/76 cm length of tape in half. Sew these handles securely to the WS of the lining. Sl lining into the knitted bag with WS tog. Sl st lining in place around facing.

Bookstore Tote Chart

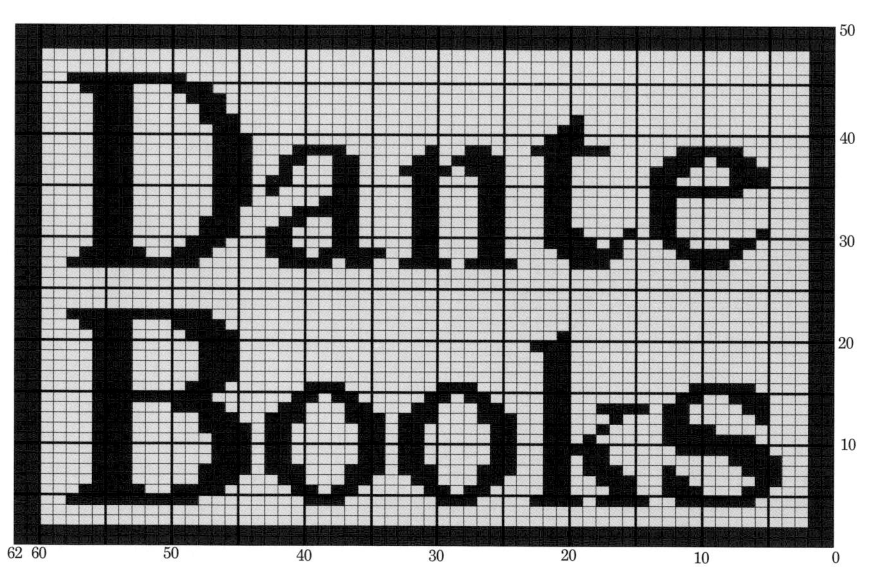

Alphabet Baby Blocks

Soft, cuddly, and colorful, knitted alphabet blocks are perfect toy to give as gifts to the babies and toddlers in your life. Of course as their literacy improves they may expect you to knit entire books for them, so you should probably get practicing your ABC's as well.

The pattern

You will need

Yarn

Any 100% Cotton 4 ply yarn, such as Rowan Siena 4 ply, in seven different colors

Each cube is made up of 6 squares and uses approx. 1/2 oz/14.25 g of MC and 1/4 oz/7 g of CC per square. The cubes listed here use the following combinations of colors:

[MC] Light green
[CC1] Red
[CC2] Dark blue
[CC3] Light blue
[CC4] Yellow
[CC5] Purple
[CC6] Orange

Use the first color for the background and the second color for the letter:

Cube 1

Square A: MC and CC1
Square B: CC2 and CC3
Square C: CC4 and CC5
Square D: CC1 and MC
Square E: CC6 and CC3
Square F: CC5 and CC4

Cube 2

Square G: CC3 and CC4
Square H: CC1 and CC2
Square I: MC and CC5
Square J: CC2 and CC6
Square K: CC4 and CC1
Square L: CC6 and CC3

Cube 3

Square M: CC5 and CC4
Square N: CC3 and CC6
Square O: CC1 and CC3
Square P: CC2 and MC
Square Q: CC4 and CC1
Square R: CC6 and CC2

Needles

US 1/2.25 mm needles
Tapestry needle

Other

Scissors
Custom-cut foam blocks: 3 3/4 in/9.5 cm cubed, or polyester foam stuffing

Pattern begins ▶

I
A
B

Finished size: 3¾ in/9.5 cm cubed
Gauge: 32 sts and 42 rows over 4 in/10 cm in st st on US1/2.25 mm needles
Note: Ensure that any filling or insert used is suitable and safe for infants and complies with legal safety standards, including regulations for fire safety.

Each cube is constructed from 6 squares. Each square has a st st center with a letter motif (as shown in the Baby Block Charts) and a seed stitch border. Sl the first st of each row purlwise to give a neat outer edge and to help with sewing up. Squares are joined together using invisible mattress stitch to form a cube and then stuffed with custom-cut foam or loose stuffing to maintain their shape.

Letter motif

Use the Baby Block Charts below as the basis of your design. For all other letters, simply substitute letters from the Serif Uppercase Charts featured on pages 112–13, and work so that each letter is centered horizontally over 20 sts, and vertically over 30 rows.

Lower border: Make 6 squares for one block

Starting with the seed stitch border, and the desired Baby Block Chart, work the border as follows:

Using background color, CO 31 sts.

Row 1 (RS): Sl 1 purlwise, * k1, p1; rep from * to end.
Rows 2–5: Rep row 1.

Middle section

Working the central section of the square in st st following relevant letter chart and maintaining 4 sts of seed stitch at beg and end of each row, cont as follows:

Row 6 (WS): Sl 1 purlwise, k1, p1, k1, p in patt to last 4 sts, k1, p1, k1, p1.
Row 7 (RS): Sl 1 purlwise, k1, p1, k in patt to last 3 sts, p1, k1, p1. These 2 rows set border patt and st st lettter motif panel.
Row 8 and all even row numbers (WS): Rep row 6.
Row 9 and all odd row numbers (RS): Rep row 7.

Cont following the chart back and forth in rows and working with alternative colors as indicated until a total of 34 rows have been worked from cast-on edge.

Top border

Row 35: Using background color only, sl 1 purlwise, * k1, p1; rep from * to end.
Rows 36–38: Rep row 35.

BO in seed stitch patt.

Finishing

Weave in ends and block or press pieces according to ball band. Join the side seams using mattress stitch, leaving a gap to insert the foam block or loose filling. Insert the filling, and close rem seams.

Baby Block Charts

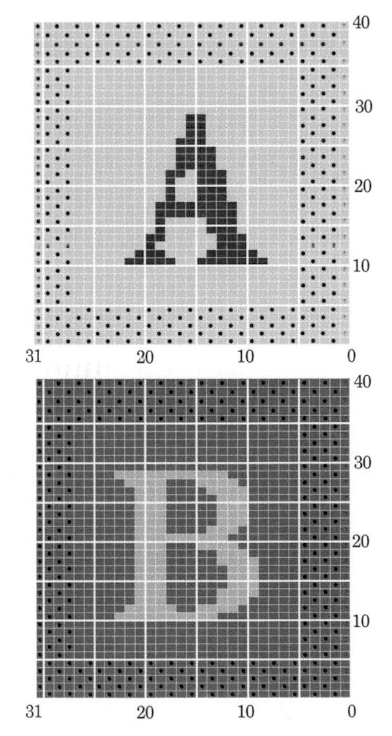

3 Slab Serif

Slab serif is a serif typeface that utilizes blocky, thick serifs, making a bold statement particularly suited for headlines. Typewriter fonts like Courier fall into this group, as do well-known advertising fonts including Rockwell and Playbill (discussed in chapter 6), and in-text fonts with a bold appeal like Clarendon and Egyptienne. There are a wide variety of slab serif fonts, but their common denominators are chunky, thick serifs and striking visual appeal.

The slab serif has its origins in advertising. A typeface with strong, bold lines was needed for headlines, ad copy, and posters. Slab serifs were perfect because of their clear impact. A craze for all things Egyptian arose in western Europe during the nineteenth century, and although in actuality the slab serif typeface had nothing in common with ancient Egyptian letter forms, it came to be associated with Egypt in the public eye due to heavy advertising and marketing linking the two. In fact, many of the early slab serif fonts were named after cities in Egypt.

Today, slab serifs are most widely associated with lettering used in American sportswear and college garments. This connection is used to great effect in the Child's Initialed Backpack (facing page) and the Letterman Sweater (page 57). The Slab Serif Charts in this book (pages 116–17) include uppercase letters only, as is traditional with this typeface. Use slab serif fonts in your own knitting when you want to make a bold statement with unequivocal impact.

Child's Initialed Backpack

Nothing has more cred on the playground than a backpack knitted in a child's favorite colors and personalized with his own initials. The bag's contents are kept safe by the drawstring closure, which is also connected to the adjustable straps.

The pattern

Finished size: 10 in/25.5 cm by 9½ in/23.5 cm
Gauge: approx 22 sts and 28 rows over 4 in/10 cm in st st on US 6/4 mm knitting needles

You will need

Yarn

Sublime Cashmere Merino silk DK (75% extra fine merino/20% silk/5% cashmere, approx. 127 yd/116 m per 1¾ oz/50 g)
[MC] Marmalade (shade 224), 2 balls
[CC] Captain Peacock (shade 163), 1 ball

Needles

US 6/4 mm knitting needles
US 2.5/3 mm DPNs for I-cord straps
Tapestry needle

Other

Scissors
Safety pin
Fabric for lining, 20 in/50 cm square
Sewing thread and needle

Letter motif

Use the Initials Chart on page 55. If substituting initials, use a maximum of 2 letters from the Slab Serif Charts on pages 116–17. Arrange so that there is a 2 st gap between your chosen letters and so that the letters are then centered horizontally over the 56 st space. If using letters that require more or fewer sts than the letters "L" and "T," work more or fewer sts either side of the letters so that they are centered.

Front

Using MC and US 6/4 mm needles, CO 56 sts.

Starting with a k row, work in st st until piece measures 4 in/10 cm, ending with a p row.

Next row (RS): K15 in MC, with CC work letter "T" from Initials Chart using the intarsia method, k2 in MC, with CC work letter "L" from Initials Chart using the intarsia method, k15 in MC.
Next row (WS): P15 in MC, with CC work letter "L" from Initials Chart, p2 in MC, with CC work letter "T" from Initials Chart, p15 in MC.
Rep prev 2 rows, working through Initials Charts until letters are complete.

Using MC, work in st st for a further 3 in/8 cm ending with a WS row. ▶

Next row (RS): * K1, p1, rep from * to end to form 1x1 rib.
Rep prev row a further 5 times.

Next row: Purl.
Work 1x1 rib for a further 6 rows.

BO knitwise.

Back

Using MC and US 6/4 mm needles, CO 56 sts. Starting with a k row work in st st until piece measures 9½ in/24 cm, ending with a p row.

Change to 1x1 rib, and work for 6 rows.

Next row: Purl.

Work 1x1 rib for a further 6 rows.

BO knitwise.

Straps (make 2)

Using CC and US 2.5/3 mm DPNs, CO 4 sts.

With working yarn at left end of needle, k4 from right end of needle to begin I-cord.

Swap needles between hands but *do not turn* needle, slide sts to right end of needle and, with working yarn at left end of sts, k4.

Rep prev steps until I-cord measures 46 in/117 cm, break yarn, and draw through 4 sts with yarn needle to close.

Finishing

Weave in ends and block pieces according to ball band, and allow to dry before seaming.

On the front piece, fold down the ribbed section at the p row, and hem to WS of piece. Rep for back piece.

Attach a safety pin to one end of the I-cord. Pin the front and back pieces tog with WS facing. With front facing, draw the I-cord with the safety pin attached to it from right to left through the hem of front piece, then, with back facing, draw the I-cord through the hem from right to left, using the safety pin to work the cord through.

Remove the safety pin and attach it to one end of the second I-cord. With front facing, draw I-cord through hem from left to right, then with back facing, draw the cord through hem from left to right again.

Adjust the cords so that they are even. The cords should now be placed so that when the tails are pulled away from the bag, the top draws closed.

Seam both sides using mattress stitch, inserting and attaching cords to the inside of the bag approx. 1½ in/4 cm from the bottom of the pieces. Graft the bottom edges of the pieces tog using the grafting technique (page 20). Draw yarn ends to the inside of the bag and weave in.

Lining

Cut the fabric into two 10 in/25 cm square pieces. Place and pin hemmed pieces of fabric tog. Using ½ in/1 cm seam allowances, sew around three sides, leaving one side open. Fold down ½ in/1 cm of the fabric at open edge, press and hem. Insert lining into backpack and sew to inside of bag.

Initials Chart

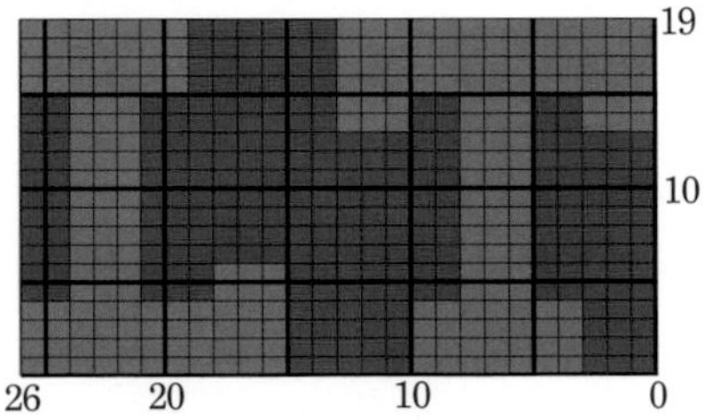

M

Letterman Sweater

This classic letterman sweater is perfect for the varsity player in your life, or as a Halloween costume. Knit it in the school colors of your choice.

The pattern

Sizes	S	M	L	XL
To fit chest	36 in 91 cm	40 in 102 cm	44 in 112 cm	48 in 122 cm
Finished chest measurement	40 in 102 cm	44 in 112 cm	48 in 122 cm	52 in 132 cm
Length	25½ in 64.5 cm	26¾ in 68 cm	27¼ in 69 cm	27¾ in 70.5 cm
Sleeve length	18 in 45.5 cm	18½ in 47 cm	19½ in 49.5 cm	20 in 50.5 cm
Yarn				
[MC] Claret (shade 777) [CC] Aran (shade 776)	9 balls 5 balls	10 balls 6 balls	11 balls 7 balls	12 balls 8 balls

Gauge: approx. 18 sts and 24 rows over 4 in/10 cm in st st using US 7/4.5 mm needles

Letter motif patch

Use the Varsity Letter Chart on page 59. If substituting a letter, use the Slab Serif Charts on pages 116–17. On the chart of your chosen letter, draw a box around the letter that is 21 sts wide and 17 rows high, making sure the letter is in the center. If your letter has an even number of sts, one side will have 1 st extra.

Using CC and US 7/4.5 mm needles, CO 21 sts and starting with a k row work 2 rows in st st. ▶

You will need

Yarn

King Cole Merino Blend Aran (medium-weight, 100% wool, 88 yds/80 m per 1¾ oz/50 g ball)
See table above for shades and quantities.

Needles

US 5/3.75 mm knitting needles
US 7/4.5 mm knitting needles
Tapestry needle

Other

Scissors
Stitch holder

Commence Varsity Tote Chart

Using stranding technique and working in st st, work rows 1–19 of the letter chart.

Using CC, work 3 rows in st st.

BO.

Back

Using MC and US 5/3.75 mm needles, CO 91 [101, 109, 119] sts.

Row 1 (RS): K1, * p1, k1; rep from * to end.
Row 2 (WS): P1, * k1, p1; rep from * to end.
These 2 rows form the rib.

Cont in rib, working the stripe sequence as follows: 2 rows CC, 4 rows MC, 2 rows CC, 4 rows MC.

Change to US 7/4.5 mm needles and, using MC only, starting with a k row, work in st st until back measures 15½ [16, 16¼, 16½] in/39 [41, 41.5, 42] cm, ending with a p row.

Shape armholes

Cont in st st and *at the same time* BO 3 [4, 4, 5] sts at beg of next 2 rows.

Dec 1 st at each end of next 3 [4, 5, 6] rows.
79 [85, 91, 97] sts

Cont in st st without shaping until armhole measures 9 [9½, 10, 10¼] in/23 [24, 25.5, 26] cm, ending with a p row.

Shape shoulders

BO 8 [9, 10, 10] sts at beg of next 4 rows.
47 [49, 51, 57] sts

BO 8 [8, 8, 10] sts at beg of next 2 rows.
31 [33, 35, 37] sts

BO.

Front

Shape Shoulders

Work as given for back until front is 14 [14, 16, 18] rows less than back, ending with a p row 79 [85, 91, 97] sts.

Shape left side of neck

Next row (RS): K34 [36, 39, 41] and turn, leaving rem sts on stitch holder.
Dec 1 st at neck edge on next 10 [10, 11, 11] rows.
24 [26, 28, 30] sts
Work 3 [3, 4, 6] rows without shaping, ending with a p row.

Shape left shoulder

BO 8 [9, 10, 10] sts at beg of next and foll alt row.
8 [8, 8, 10] sts

BO.

Shape right side of neck

Sl center 11 [13, 13, 15] sts onto a stitch holder.

With RSF rejoin yarn to rem 34 [36, 39, 41] sts, k to end.

Dec 1 st at neck edge on next 10 [10, 11, 11] rows.
24 [26, 28, 30] sts

Work 4 [4, 5, 7] rows without shaping, ending with a k row.

Shape right shoulder

BO 8 [9, 10, 10] sts at beg of next and foll alt row.
8 [8, 8, 10] sts

BO.

Sleeves (both)

Using MC and US 5/3.75 mm needles, CO 41 [43, 45, 47] sts and work in striped rib as given for back. Change to US 7/4.5 mm needles and using MC only, starting with a k row work 2 rows in st st.

Shape sleeves

Inc 1 st at each end of next and every foll fourth row to 83 [87, 91, 93] sts.

Cont without shaping until sleeve measures 18 [18½, 19½, 20] in/45.5 [47, 49.5, 50.5] cm, ending with a p row.

Shape top

BO 3 [4, 4, 5] sts at beg of next 2 rows. *77 [79, 83, 83] sts*

Dec 1 st at each end of next and every foll alt row to 71 sts.

BO 12 sts at beg of next 2 rows, then 14 sts at beg of next 2 rows.

BO rem 19 sts.

Neckband

Weave in ends and block or press the pieces according to the instructions on the ball band.

Join right shoulder seam. With RSF, using MC and US 5/3.75 mm needles, pick up and k20 [20, 22, 24] sts down left side of neck, k across 11 [13, 13, 15] sts at center front, pick up and k 20 [20, 22, 24] sts up right side of neck, and 31 [33, 35, 37] sts across back of neck. *82 [86, 92, 100] sts*

Next row: * K1, p1; rep from * to end.

Rep this row working stripe sequence as follows: 2 rows CC, 2 rows MC, 2 rows CC, 1 row MC.

Using MC only, BO loosely in rib.

Finishing

Join left shoulder and neckband seam. Mark center of sleeve top and sew sleeve into armhole, matching mark to shoulder seam. Join sleeve seam. Join side seam.

Pin letter motif in position on left side of front and sew in place.

Varsity Letter Chart

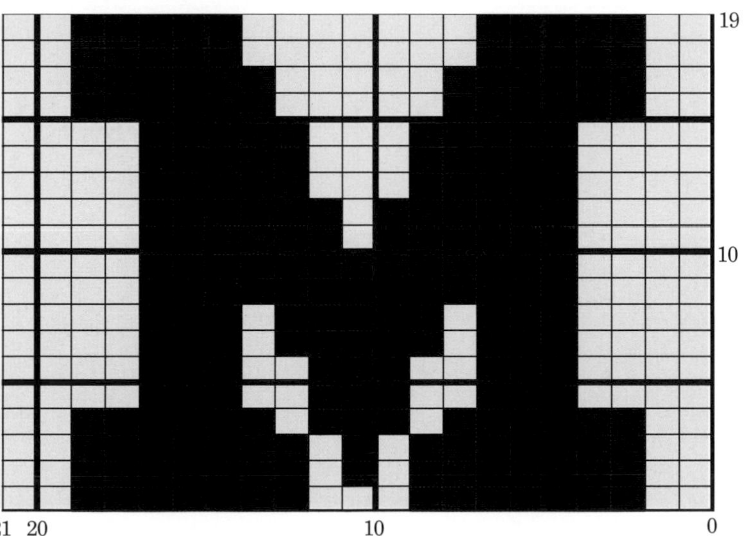

4 STENCIL

The stencil typeface group is an ornamental group (discussed in more detail in chapter 6) most obviously associated with shipping crates and army gear. It was created for print relatively recently, in the 1930s, and was made specifically to imitate hand-stenciled, often spray-painted letters. Unlike the widely used typeface groups discussed so far, a stencil font is most often used sparingly for a fun, novelty appeal. Stencil fonts tend to be named after military terms, like Top Secret or Covert Ops, or to denote shipping usage, like Crate or Cargo. Stencil fonts are best known for their usage in easily recognized titles for the TV shows *M*A*S*H* and *The A-Team*.

The printed versions of these fonts often include fanciful touches like "spray-painted" edges or camouflage incorporated into the negative space. When using these fonts in knitting, a more straightforward approach is necessary. The stencil charts in this book are more traditional, based on the original stencil font called, appropriately enough, Stencil, which was designed for Ludlow Typograph by R. Hunter Middleton in 1937. In the "CAFE" French Press Cozy (facing page) and Toy Tidy Bag (page 65), the stencil font is used to excellent effect. In your own projects, you can use the Stencil Charts (pages 118–19) to make items that have connotations of identification, the military, or shipping.

"CAFE" French Press Cozy

A good introduction to stranded colorwork, this easy rectangular project will help keep your coffee warm during those long, lazy weekend mornings. It's styled after the burlap sacks your beans were shipped over in.

The pattern

Finished size: approx. 11 in/28 cm by 4½ in/11.5 cm
Gauge: approx. 27 sts and 35 rows over 4 in/10 cm in st st on US 2/3 mm needles

Letter motif

Use the "CAFE" Chart on page 63. If changing the wording, use the Stencil Charts on pages 118–19. You can use a maximum of 4 letters, and with 1 st gaps between them, these cannot exceed 61 sts. Center your word over the 71-st st st space, plus 4 seed sts either side at the point in the patt where the chart commences.

The Cozy

Using US 3/3 mm needles and MC, CO 79 sts.

Row 1 (RS): (K1, p1) to last st, k1.
Rep prev row 3 more times to form seed stitch border.
Row 5: (K1, p1) twice, k to last 4 sts, (p1, k1) twice.
Row 6: (P1, k1) twice, p to last 4 sts, (k1, p1) twice.
Rep rows 5 and 6 a further three times, ending with a WS row (8 rows total).

Commence "CAFE" Chart

Work rows 1–19 of chart using the stranding and intarsia techniques.
Next row (WS): Using MC only, (p1, k1) twice, p to last 4 sts, (k1, p1) twice.
Next row: (K1, p1) twice, k to last 4 sts, (p1, k1) twice.
Rep prev 2 rows a further three times.

Work 4 rows of seed stitch border. ▶

You will need

Yarn

Rowan Pure Wool (4 ply, 137 yds/125 m per 1¾ oz/50 g ball)
[MC] Taupe (shade 00453), 1 ball
[CC] Dark Brown (shade 00417), 1 ball

Needles

US 2/3 mm needles, or size needed to obtain gauge
US D/3 mm crochet hook

Other

Scissors
3 buttons, approx. ½ in/1 cm

BO.

Crochet buttonholes

The crochet buttonhole edging can be replaced with ready-made button loops if preferred.

Using US D/3 mm hook and MC, attach to one end of short side of rectangle, ch 4, sc in same st, sc to middle of short side, ch 4, sc in same st, sc to end of side, ch 4, sc in same st. Fasten off.

Weave in ends and block or press according to ball band. Attach buttons to other short side corresponding with buttonholes.

"CAFE" Chart

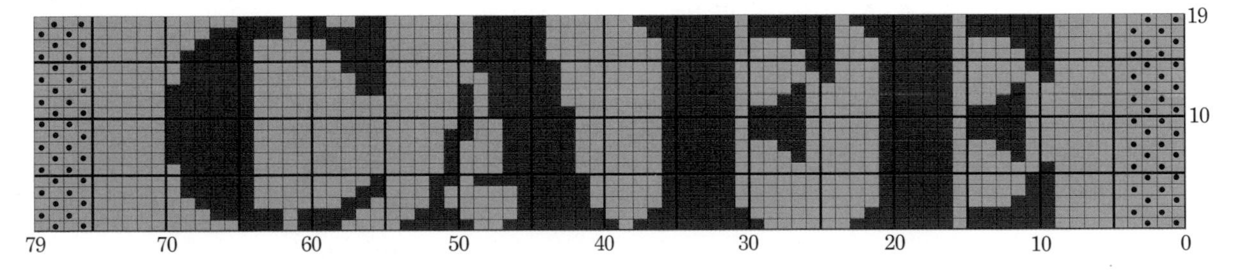

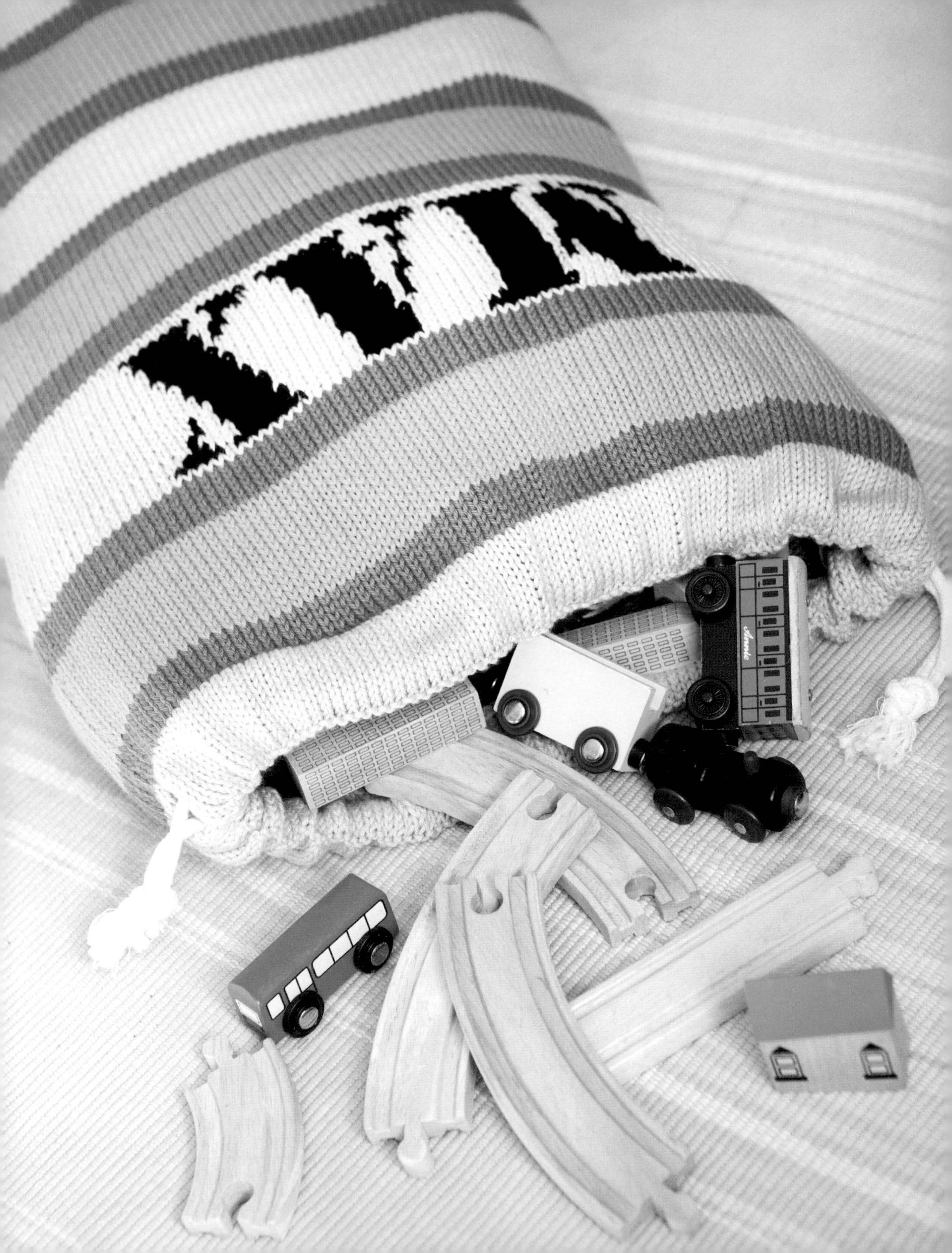

Toy Tidy Bag

It's possible—just possible —that a fun, army-style toy bag, with the toy owner's name boldly stenciled onto it, might capture the imagination of that toy owner enough to actually inspire them to put their toys back in that bag once they're done playing. We make no guarantees, but surely it's worth a try.

The pattern

Finished size: 17¼ in/44 cm by 19½ in/50 cm
Gauge: 20 sts and 28 rows over 4 in/10 cm in st st on US 6/4 mm needles
Note: Check your gauge—if fewer sts or rows, use smaller needles; if more, use larger needles.

Letter motif

Use the Stencil Charts on pages 118–19 to chart your chosen name, leaving a 1 st gap between each letter. (Use the Toy Tidy Bag Name Chart on page 66 as an example.) Draw a box 88 sts wide and 19 rows high around the charted name, making sure the name is in the center. If the name has an odd number of sts, then one side will have 1 st extra.

Bag base

Using MC, CO 16 sts.

P1 row.

Work 8 rows in st st (1 row k, 1 row p), starting with a k row. CO 6 sts at beg of first 2 rows, then 3 sts at beg of next 2 rows, and 2 sts at beg of foll 4 rows. *42 sts*
Inc 1 st at each end of next and every foll 8th row to 48 sts.

Work 3 rows without shaping. ▶

You will need

Yarn

Rowan Handknit Cotton (medium-weight, 100% cotton, 93 yd/85 m per 1¾ oz/50 g)
[MC] Celery (shade 309), 3 balls
[CC1] Gooseberry (shade 219), 2 balls
[CC2] Pesto (shade 344), 2 balls
[CC3] Black (shade 252), 1 ball

Needles

US 6/4 mm knitting needles
Tapestry needle

Other

Scissors
Cord for drawstring, 118 in/3 m

Note: As with all items using cords, this may present an entanglement hazard for very small children.

Inc 1 st at beg of next and foll alt rows to 52 sts.

Work 21 rows without shaping, ending with a p row. Dec 1 st at each end of next and foll 8th row.

Work 3 rows without shaping.

Dec 1 st at each end of next and every foll alt row to 42 sts.

Work 1 row.

BO 2 sts at beg of next 4 rows, 3 sts at beg of foll 2 rows, and 6 sts at beg of foll 2 rows.

BO rem 16 sts.

Back

Using MC, CO 88 sts.

Work in st st (starting with a k row), repeat the stripe patt (14 rows MC, 6 rows CC2, 14 rows CC1, 6 rows CC2) twice. **

Work a further 22 rows MC, 6 rows CC2, 14 rows CC1, 6 rows CC2.

Drawstring channel

Using MC, work 11 rows in st st, ending with a k row.

Next row (foldline): K to end.

Work 12 rows in st st, starting with a k row.

BO.

Front

Work as given for back to **.

Commence chart

Using MC, work 2 rows in st st.

Using MC for the background and CC3 for the name, and using stranding and intarsia techniques, work from the chart as follows:

Reading RS (k rows) from right to left and WS (p rows) from left to right, work the 88 sts from the chart beg at the lower right corner, from row 1 to row 19, where the chart is completed.

Using MC, p 1 row.

Cont in st st (starting with a k row), working 6 rows CC2, 14 rows CC1, 6 rows CC2.

Work the drawstring channel as given for back.

Finishing

Block or press the pieces according to the instructions on the ball band. Sew in all ends neatly. Sew the side edges together from lower edge up to last stripe of CC2. Leave a gap and join edges from fold line to top edge. Fold top edge to WS along foldline and sl st into place. Sew back and front around base. Cut cord in half and thread one length through the drawstring channel and around the bag, starting and ending at same gap. Knot ends of cord together. Do the same with the other length of cord through the gap on the other side.

Toy Tidy Bag Name Chart

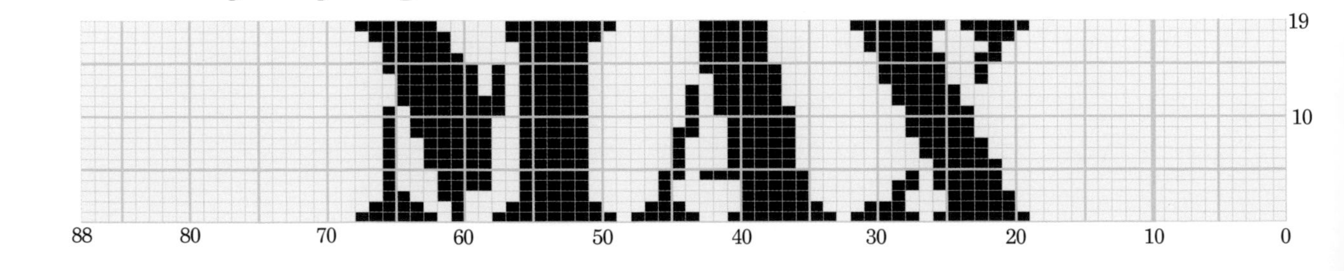

Lady's "PARIS" Sweater

The stencil typeface's combination of boldness and sharp detailing make it a strong choice for decorating any adult-size garment, particularly when used with bold, classic color combinations as in this raglan-style sweater.

The pattern

Sizes	S	M	L	XL
To fit chest	32–34 in 81–86 cm	36–38 in 91.5–96.5 cm	40–42 in 101.5–106.5 cm	44–46 in 111.5–117 cm
Finished chest measurement	38 in 96 cm	41½ in 105 cm	45¼ in 115 cm	49 in 124 cm
Length	23 in 58 cm	23 in 58 cm	24½ in 62 cm	25½ in 65 cm
Sleeve length to underarm	17 in 43 cm	17 in 43 cm	17½ in 44.5 cm	17½ in 44.5 cm
Yarn				
[MC] Marine (shade 01660) [CC1] Carmine (shade 00100) [CC2] Natural (shade 02055)	5 balls 1 ball 1 ball	6 balls 1 ball 1 ball	7 balls 1 ball 1 ball	7 balls 1 ball 1 ball

You will need

Yarn

Rowan Creative Focus Worsted (75% wool/25% alpaca, 220 yd/200 m per 3½ oz/100 g)
See table above for shades and for quantities.

Needles

US 8/5 mm knitting needles
US 7/4.5 mm knitting needles

Other

Scissors
2 stitch holders

Gauge: 17 sts and 24 rows rows over 4 in/10 cm in st st using US 8/5 mm needles ▶

Letter motif

Use the Sleeve Letters Chart on facing page. If changing the wording, use the Stencil Charts on pages 118–19. On the chart of your chosen letter, draw a box around the letter that is 16 sts wide and 19 rows high, making sure the letter is in the center. If your letter has an even number of sts, one side will have 1 st extra. Place the charts in the correct sequence vertically to make one large chart; leave 1 row in between each letter. Remember you will be working from the bottom up. You will fit a maximum of 5 letters for S and M sizes and 6 letters for L and XL sizes.

Back and front

Using MC and US 7/4.5 mm knitting needles, CO 82 [90, 98, 106] sts.

Row 1 (RS): K2, * p2, k2; rep from * to end.
Row 2 (WS): P2, * k2, p2; rep from * to end.
These 2 rows form the rib.

Cont in rib for a total of 10 rows.

Change to US 8/5 mm knitting needles and starting with a k row work in st st until back measures 16 [16, 16¼, 16½] in/40 [40, 41, 42] cm ending with a p row.

Shape armholes

BO 5 [5, 6, 6] sts at beg of next 2 rows. *72 [80, 86, 94] sts*

Dec 1 st at each end of next 3 [5, 2, 6] rows. *66 [70, 82, 82] sts*

Dec 1 st at each end of every foll alt row until 30 [30, 34, 38] sts rem.

Sl sts onto holder.

Right sleeve

Using MC and US 7/4.5 mm knitting needles, CO 46 [46, 50, 54] sts and work in rib as given for back.

Change to US 8/5 mm knitting needles and starting with a k row, work in st st for 6 rows.

Shape top
Inc 1 st at each end of next and every foll 6th row to 58 [56, 58, 60] sts, then on every 4th row until 74 [76, 78, 80] sts.

Cont without shaping until sleeve measures 17 [17, 17½, 17½] in/ 43 [43, 44.5, 44.5] cm, ending with a p row.

BO 5 [5, 6, 6] sts at beg of next 2 rows. *64 [66, 66, 68] sts*

Dec 1 st at each end of next and every foll alt row to 24 [24, 24, 24] sts.

Slip sts onto holder.

Left sleeve
Work as given for right sleeve to row 17 [17, 19, 21].

Commence Sleeve Letters Chart
Work letter "S" from chart in st st using CC1 for the letter and intarsia technique. Work rem sts of row in MC and st st.

Continue to work from chart alternating letters between CC1 and CC2 and *at the same time* maintain incs as for right sleeve.

Finishing
Weave in ends and block or press all pieces according to ball band.

Join both of the front and right back raglan seams.

Neck edging
Sl sts from holders onto US 7/4.5 mm needles and with RS facing rejoin MC 108 [108, 116, 124] sts.

K22 [22, 22, 22], (k2tog) twice, k26 [26, 30, 30], (k2tog) twice, k20 [20, 20, 20], (k2tog) twice, k to end 102 [102, 110, 118] sts.

K 3 rows.
BO.

Sew up remaining raglan sleeves and neckband.

Sleeve Letters Chart

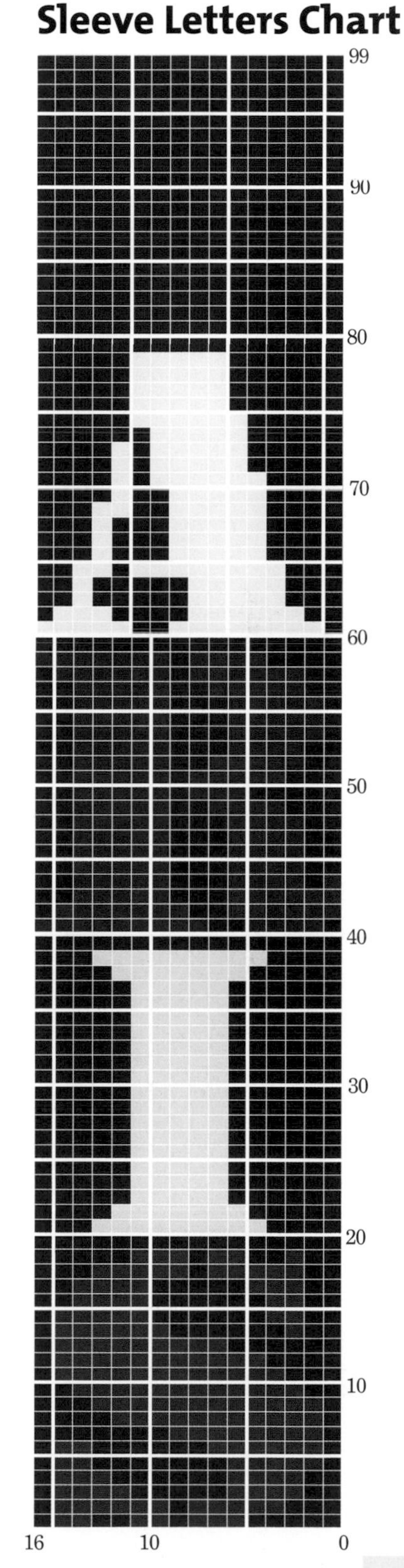

5 *Script*

The script typeface group includes fonts created to resemble the smooth, fluid lines of cursive handwriting. Script fonts have to be designed very carefully to promote readability, especially when used on-screen. They are not widely used in text, but are often used sparingly and decoratively to create a soft and feminine or classical visual appeal.

The script typeface group can be divided into two subgroups: Formal, which resembles cursive writing using a fountain pen and includes fonts like English and Kuenstler Script; and casual, which resembles less structured handwriting or calligraphy made with a brush and includes the fonts Brush Script (associated nostalgically with post-WWII America) and Mistral (still widely used today for ads and shop signage all over southern France).

When using a script font for your knitting project, there are a number of special considerations to take into account. In order for each letter to be interchangeable and to line up with its neighbors, you may choose to make sure that each letter starts and ends at the same stitch or row position for every letter, so that it looks like the letters join. The letters also slant, so when making charts, the space around each letter will need to overlap. When using these charts, it's a good idea to trace the letters that you want (in the order that you need) onto a new chart and place them so that they join in the way you want them to. This will enable you to show the sophisticated, sweeping curves and to capture the details.

Users of the Script Charts (pages 120–25) can choose to link up their letters or just keep them closely spaced, as in the "Amour" Heart Pillow (facing page). Either way, the script charts are carefully designed to promote readability while providing an elegant, feminine touch.

"Amour" Heart Pillow

An elegant addition to any home, this heart-shaped pillow can be made in any color combination to suit your décor. The script lettering provides a feminine touch that enhances the romantic nature of the project.

The pattern

Finished size: approx. 14 in/35.5 cm by 13 in/33 cm
Gauge: 27 sts and 35 rows over 4 in/10 cm in st st on US 2/3 mm knitting needles

Letter motif

Use the "Amour" Chart on page 73. If changing the wording, use the Script Lowercase Charts on pages 124–25. You will be able to fit a maximum of 5 or 6 letters within the 59 st space. Note that there should be no spaces between letters. If your chosen word is less than 59 sts, remember to center your word horizontally over the total number of sts (97) at the point in the patt where the chart commences.

Front

Using MC, CO 3 sts.

Row 1 (RS): Knit.
Row 2 (WS): Purl.
Row 3: K1, m1, k to last st, m1, k1. *2 sts inc*
Row 4: Purl.
Rep rows 3 and 4 until you have 97 sts. **
Work 4 rows in st st without incs ending on a WS row.

Commence "Amour" Chart

Using MC and CC as shown in the chart, work rows 1–13 of chart using stranding and intarsia techniques.

Using MC only, work 7 rows in st st ending with a WS row. ▶

You will need

Yarn

Debbie Bliss Baby Cashmerino (55% wool/ 33% microfiber/12% cashmere, 137 yds/ 125 m per 1¾ oz/50 g ball)
[MC] Dark Teal (shade 0072), 3 balls
[CC] Light Teal (shade 0073), 1 ball

Needles

US 2/3 mm knitting needles
Tapestry needle

Other

Scissors
Stitch holder
Heart-shaped pillow form, 13¾ in/35 cm

amour

Top of heart

Next Row (RS): K48, turn, leaving rem 49 sts on stitch holder.

Row 2: Purl.

Row 3: K1, (ssk) twice, k to last 5 sts, (k2tog) twice, k1. *2 sts dec*

Row 4: Purl.

Rep previous two rows until 16 sts rem.

BO.

With RSF rejoin yarn to rem 49 sts and work 2 rows in st st.

Work decs as above until 17 sts rem.

BO.

Back

Work as for front to **.

Starting with a k row work in st st without incs for 22 rows, ending with a WS row.

Work top of heart as for front.

Weave in ends and block or press according to ball band.

Finishing

Sew pieces together using mattress st and insert the pillow form at the halfway point before closing seam.

"Amour" Chart

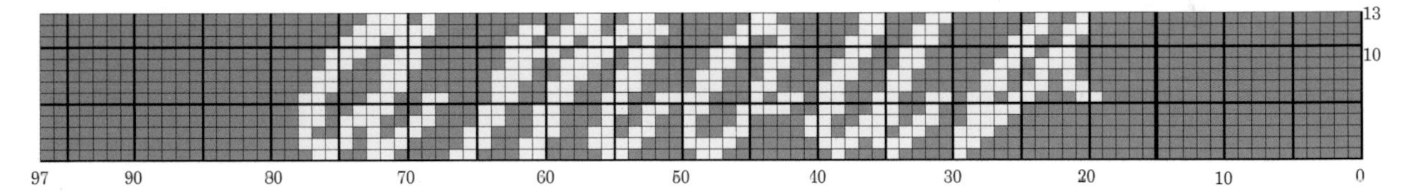

Girl's Dress

This cute dress can be personalized with any name or word, and with the little princess's favorite colors, using the elegant script font.

The pattern

Sizes	12–18 months	18–24 months	24–36 months
To fit chest	23 in 59 cm	24½ in 62 cm	26 in 65 cm
Finished chest measurement	23½ in 50 cm	25 in 63 cm	26 in 66 cm
Length	16½ in 42 cm	17½ in 44 cm	18 in 46 cm
Yarn			
[MC] Windsor (shade 849)	2 balls	2 balls	3 balls
[CC1] Green Slate (shade 844)	2 balls	2 balls	3 balls
[CC2] Bubbles (shade 724)	1 ball	1 ball	1 ball
[CC3] Poppy (shade 741)	1 ball	1 ball	1 ball

You will need

Yarn
Rowan Cotton Glacé (100% cotton, approx. 125 yds/115 m per 1¾ oz/50 g)
See table above for shades and quantities.

Needles
US 3/3.25 mm knitting needles
US 2/3 mm knitting needles
Tapestry needle

Other
Scissors
Stitch holder
1 small button

Pattern begins ▶

Gauge: approx. 23 sts and 32 rows over 4 in/10 cm in st st using US 3/3.25 mm needles
Size shown: 24–36 months

Letter motif

Use the Script Lowercase Charts on pages 124–25 to create your chosen name or word. On the chart of your chosen letter, draw a box around the chosen letter that fits exactly to its width and height. The maximum number of letters that will fit all sizes is 6 or 7.

Place all your letters side by side horizontally. The graph starts on row 17 and the last sts of this first row should end 6 sts in from the outer edge. The starting position of the word will depend on the amount of letters you have chosen to use. Use the "Bella" Chart provided (facing page) as a guide.

Back

Using US 2/3 mm needles and CC2, CO 90 [98, 106] sts.

Row 1 (RS): Knit.
Row 2 (WS): Knit.
These 2 rows form the garter st patt.

Change to MC and work in garter st for a further 6 rows.

Change to US 3/3.25 mm needles and CC1, and starting with a k row, work 2 rows in st st, change to MC, and work 2 rows in st st. Maintain this stripe sequence throughout.

Dec 1 st at each end of the next and every foll 8th row until 68 [72, 76] sts, then work straight until work measures 13 [13¾, 14½] in/33 [35, 37] cm.

Shape armholes and divide for back neck

BO 4 [4, 4] sts at beg of next 2 rows 60 [64, 68] sts.

BO 3 [3, 3] sts on the foll 2 rows 54 [58, 62] sts.

Dec 1 st at edge, k until 26 [30, 34] sts on RH needle, turn, and leave rem sts on holder. Work each side of neck separately.

Dec 1 st at armhole edge on next 2 [2, 2] rows, then on next 2 [2, 2] k rows, and the foll 4th row 21 [25, 29] sts.

Work until armhole measures 4¼ [4½, 4¾] in/ 11 [11.5, 12] cm ending on a k row.

Shape back neck

BO 10 [14, 18] sts, dec 1 st at neck edge on next 3 [3, 3] rows. *8 [10, 12] sts*

Work 1 row more.

BO.

Slip sts from holder back to needle and with RSF, rejoin yarn and work to match left side.

Front

Work as back to end of row 16.

Commence chart

Maintaining stripe sequence and shaping as set for back, using intarsia technique and CC2, work rows 1–26 of chart.

Cont as set for back until armhole shaping is complete.

Dec 1 st at each end of next 3 [3, 3] rows, then next 2 [2, 2] k rows, then on foll fourth row. *42 [50, 58] sts*

Cont straight in st st until 6 rows less than back.

Shape front neck

K 14 [16, 18], turn, leaving rem sts on hold. Cont on these 14 [16, 18] sts.

BO 4 sts at neck edge, then dec 1 st at neck edge until 8 [10, 12] sts rem.

Maintaining stripe sequence, work rows to match back armhole.

With RSF, rejoin yarn to rem sts and BO 14 [18, 22] sts, then work to match left side.

Sew shoulder seams tog.

Back neck opening

Using size US 2/3 mm needles and CC2, pick up and k23 [25, 27] sts down right back neck and k23 [25, 27] sts up left neck opening. *46 [50, 54] sts*

BO 22 [24, 26] sts, (k2tog, BO 1 st), BO rem sts to end.

Neck edge

Using size US 2/3 mm needles and CC2, starting at back neck opening pick up and k15 [17, 19] sts to shoulder, 10 sts down left front neck 14 [18, 22] sts across front neck 10 sts up to shoulder; 15 [17, 19] sts to center back neck. *64 [72, 80] sts*

K2 rows.

BO.

Armhole edging

Using US 2/3 mm needles and CC3, pick up and k32 [34, 36] sts up to shoulder seam, then 32 [34, 36] sts down to armhole edge. *64 [68, 72] sts*

K2 rows.

BO.

Finishing

Weave in ends and block or press to finished size according to ball band.

Sew up the side seams. Make a button loop at the top opening on the right back, and sew on a button to match.

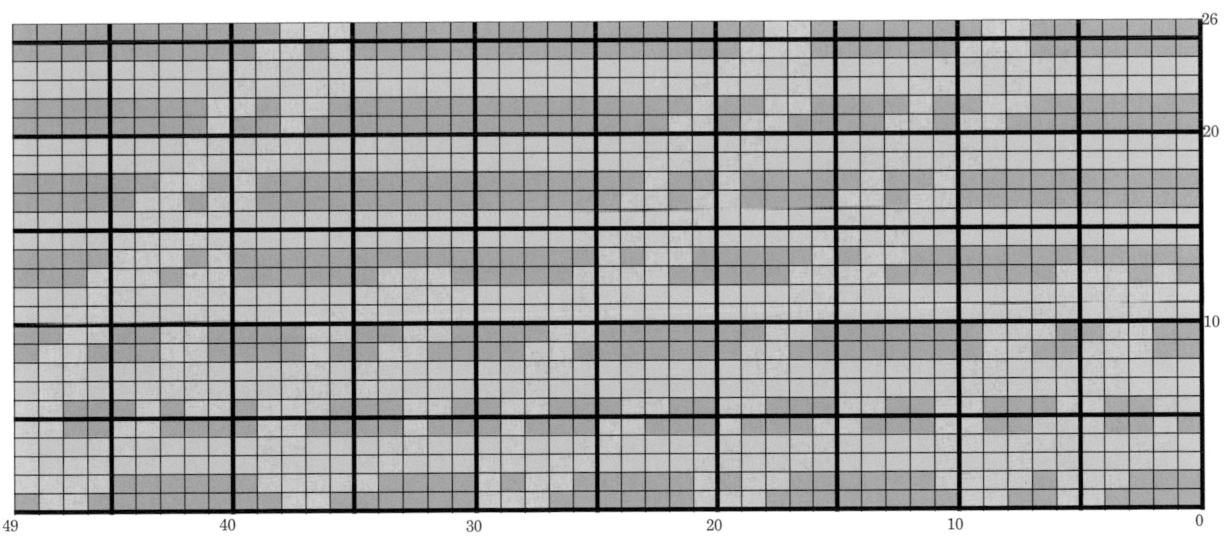

Mobius Twist Scarf

Rather than simply spelling out a name, word, or message, ornate fonts like the script typeface can be used purely for decoration and pattern, as in this twisted scarf, which, like the letters themselves, follows a graceful curve.

The pattern

Finished size: approx. 12 in/30 cm by 51 in/130 cm
Gauge: 20 sts and 26 rows over 4 in/10 cm in st st on US 7/4.5 mm needles

Letter motif

The pattern on this scarf is added using duplicate st (see page 23) after the main fabric has been created. This means that you can add any selection of letters from the Script Charts on pages 120–25, or use the selection of character charts included on the facing page. Draw a box around your choice of characters and, using a selection of colors, work in your letters randomly on the mobius twist scarf fabric.

Basic twist scarf

Using MC and US 7/4.5 mm needles, CO 43 sts.

Row1 (RS): Knit.
Row2 (WS): K3, p to 3 sts before end, k3.
Repeat prev 2 rows a further 166 times until work measures approx. 51 in/130 cm.

BO.

Use duplicate st to add your chosen letters using contrast colors.

Finishing

Sew in loose ends and block or press to finished size according to ball band. Twist scarf. With RS and WS tog, sew up cast-on and bound-off edges. Press seam.

You will need

Yarn

Rowan Creative Focus Worsted
(75% wool/25% alpaca, 220 yd/200 m per 3½ oz/100 g)
[MC] Nickel (shade 00401), 2 balls
[CC1] Delft (shade 01321), 1 ball
[CC2] Magenta (shade 01890), 1 ball
[CC3] Carmine (shade 02055), 1 ball
[CC4] Saffron (shade 03810), 1 ball
[CC5] Ebony (shade 00500), 1 ball
[CC6] Natural (shade 00100), 1 ball
[CC7] Deep Rose (shade 02755), 1 ball

Needles

US 7/4.5 mm needles
Tapestry needle

Other

Scissors

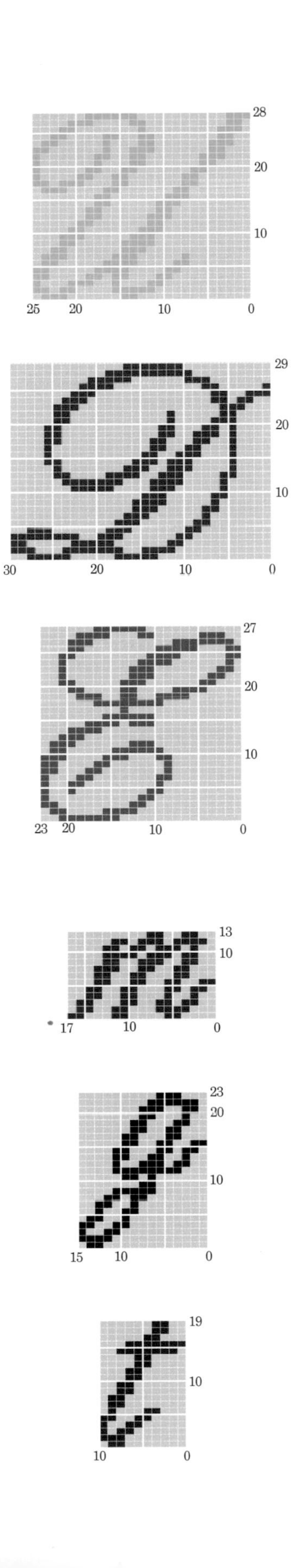
28
20
10
25 20 10 0
29
20
10
30 20 10 0
27
20
10
23 20 10 0
13
10
17 10 0
23
20
10
15 10 0
19
10
10 0

6 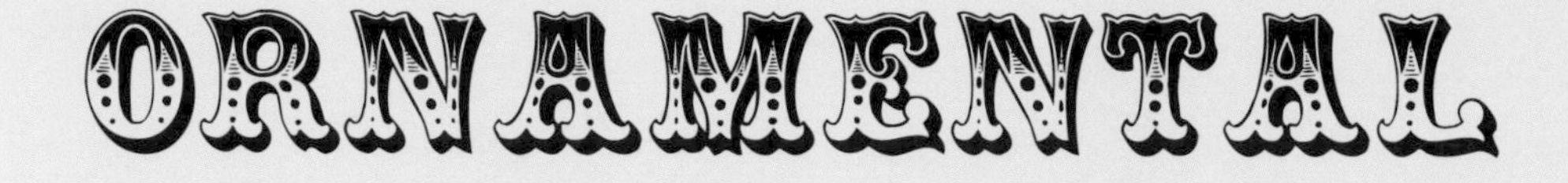

As a typeface group, "ornamental" grows even larger and more varied on an almost daily basis. However, what all the fonts included in the group have in common is that they are used exclusively for decorative purposes and to evoke a specific connotation or feeling: The Wild West, horror, illuminated manuscript lettering, circus, etc. They are considered "display types" only, meaning that they are not suitable for use at smaller sizes and in blocks of text; rather, they are used for headers, advertisements, and novelty printing. Though in the days of metal printmaking, display type and ornamental type had different meanings (involving the physical process of inking printing plates), today, in the digital typeface design age, the terms are used interchangeably (if somewhat incorrectly).

Ornamental is a loosely organized group that does not adhere to traditional typeface group rules: It contains both serif and sans serif fonts, both clean "modern" letterforms like Bodoni and those typefaces that are so fancy or over-elaborate they border on unreadable. The history of ornamental type in popular usage can be traced to the Victorian era and the industrial revolution; indeed, many of the still-used circus-type fonts strongly connote this era.

The two fonts of the ornamental group included in this book are a western font (based on Rio Oro), which will give your knitting that Wild West feel, as in the Neckerchief (page 84), and a circus font (based on Coffee Tin), which is a typeface used beautifully in the Baby Blanket (facing page). Both fonts provide an elaborately decorative touch and will make a great impact in your knitted projects.

Baby Blanket

The bold, intricate, and beautiful circus font needs a big canvas and bright color in order to show off its full impact. What better use could it be put to than to announce the name of a new little one, while also keeping him or her warm?

The pattern

Finished size: 30 in/75 cm by 40 in/100 cm
Gauge: 20 sts and 24 rows over 4 in/10 cm in st st on US 8/5 mm needles

Letter motif

Use the Baby Blanket Letter Charts and Diamond Chart on page 82. If substituting letters, use the Circus Charts on pages 126–30. It is not recommended that more than 3 letters are used, so you may want to use inititals instead of a full name.

Border

Using MC, CO 150 sts.

Work in garter st (k every row) for 10 rows.

Body of blanket

Row 1 (RS): Knit.
Row 2 (WS): K5, p to last 5 sts, k5.
These 2 rows set patt.
Work in patt as set for 1 in/2.5 cm.

Commence Diamond Chart

Work Diamond Chart using CC1 and the intarsia technique as follows:

Next row (RS): K23, work Diamond Chart, k90, work Diamond Chart, k23.
Row 2 (WS): K5, p18, work Diamond Chart, p90, work Diamond Chart, p18, k5.
Rep rows 1 and 2 until diamonds are complete. ▶

You will need

Yarn

Rico Design Essentials Soft Merino Aran (100% merino wool, 109 yd/100 m per 1¾ oz/50 g)
[MC] Light Gray (shade 020), 8 balls
[CC1] Brick Red (shade 007), 2 balls
[CC2] Yellow Ochre (shade 0642), 1 ball

Needles

US 8/5 mm circular knitting needles of at least 32 in/80 cm length
Tapestry needle

Other

Scissors

Work 3 rows in patt as set with MC, ending with a WS row.

Commence Baby Blanket Letters Chart

Beg first letter—as you are working from the bottom of the blanket upward, the first letter worked should be the last letter in the name or initials.

Row 1 (RS): Knit. Work letter so that it is centered on the row. (If using letter "M" for "TOM," k47, work letter "M" chart, k48. As the letter "M" has an odd number of sts, one side will have 1 st more than the other.)
Row 2 (WS): K5, p to last 5 sts working Baby Blanket Letter Chart as set, p5.
Rep rows 1 and 2 until 54 rows of letters are complete.

Work 2 rows in patt as set with MC.
Rep instructions for Diamond Chart.

Work 3 rows in patt as set with MC, ending with a WS row.

Work second letter as outlined above for the first letter. (If using letter "O" for "TOM," k56, work letter "O" chart, k56.)

When second letter is complete, work 2 rows with MC as set.

Rep instructions for Diamond Chart as above.

Work 3 rows in patt as set with MC ending with a WS row.

Work third letter as outlined above. (If using letter "T" for "TOM," k57, work letter "T" chart, k57.)

Work 2 rows in patt MC as set.

Rep instructions for Diamond Chart.

Work in patt as set with MC as set for a further 1 in/2.5 cm.

Work 10 rows of garter st.

BO.

Finishing

Weave in ends and block or press to finished size according to ball band instructions.

Diamond Chart

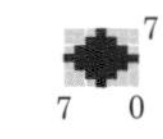

Baby Blanket Letter Charts

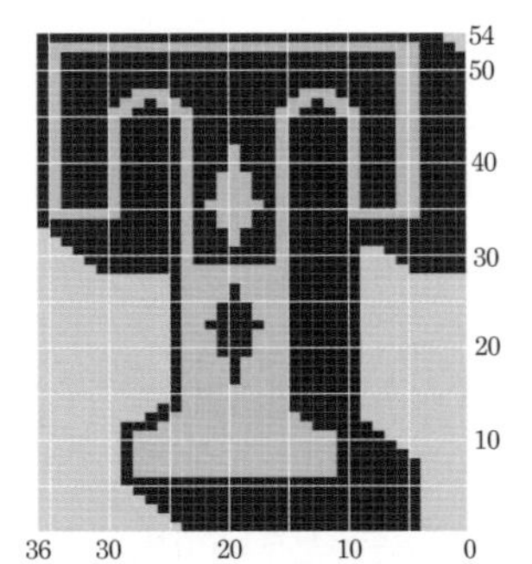

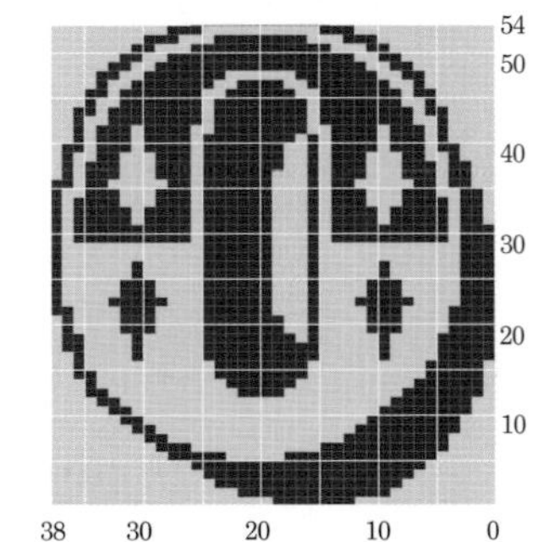

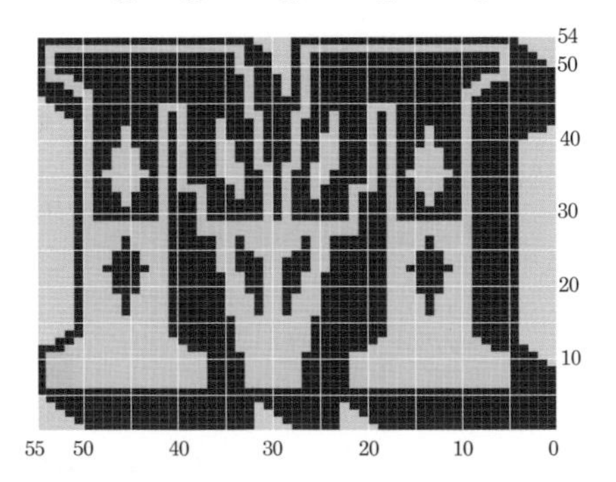

Neckerchief

Styled as a hybrid between an old-style poncho and a chic modern scarf, this neckerchief showcases what can be achieved when attractive yarns, a stylish typeface, and fine finishing are brought together.

The pattern

Finished size: 33½ in/85 cm by 18½ in/47 cm
Gauge: 21 sts to 32 rows over 4 in/10 cm in st st on US 5/3.75 mm needles

Letter motif

Use the Neckerchief Chart on the facing page. If you are changing the wording, use the Western Charts on pages 131–32. You will be able to fit a maximum of 5 letters onto the neckerchief. Draw a box 1 st wider than your chosen letters to show you the amount of space you have between each letter. The word starts on row 111 of the patt. Make sure the placement of the word is centered before you begin knitting.

Neckerchief

Using MC, CO 3 sts.

Starting with a k row, work 2 rows in st st then inc 1 st at each end of every k row as follows:

Row 3 (RS): K1, m1, k1, m1, k1. *2 sts inc*
Row 4 (WS): Purl.
Rep prev 2 rows until you have 111 sts.

Commence Neckerchief Chart

Cont incs every k row as set and *at the same time* k19 and commence chart using CC1 and intarsia technique. Work rows 1–27 of chart. *139 sts*

Cont inc as set in st st until you have 157 sts.

You will need

Yarn

Rowan Felted Tweed DK (50% merino wool/25% alpaca/25% viscose, 191 yd/175 m per 1¾ oz/50 g)
[MC] Seafarer (shade 170), 3 balls
[CC1] Clay (shade 177), 1 ball
[CC2] Duck Egg (shade 173), 1 ball

Needles

US 5/3.75 mm circular needles, 40 in/100 cm long

Other

Scissors

Change to CC2, and maintaining inc work 5 rows in garter st ending with a RS row. *163 sts*

BO.

Right border

With RSF and using CC2, pick up and k114 sts along the edge.

Work 1 row in garter st, then inc 1 st every RS row until you have 118 sts, ending with a RS row.

BO.

Left border

Work as given for right border but pick up and k120 sts. Inc as for right border until you have 124 sts.

BO.

Finishing

Weave in ends and block or press to dimensions according to ball band instructions.

Neckerchief Chart

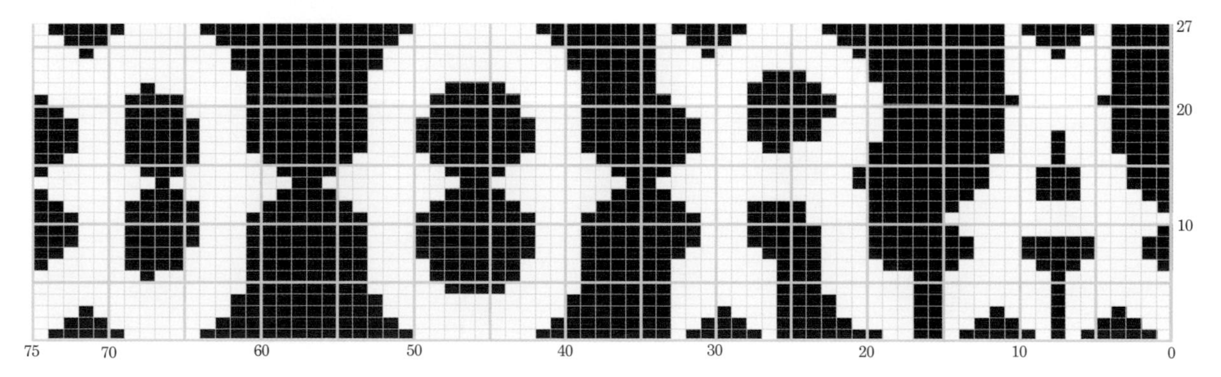

7 Black Letter

This typeface group includes the oldest mass-produced movable type (interchangeable letters made to be rearranged and reused in a printing press) in the world. Johannes Gutenberg invented the printing press and movable type in around 1455, and in doing so he changed the course of world history. Movable type made the written word affordable to a much larger segment of the population than ever before.

Gutenberg's Textura black letter was the very first font in the world. To the untrained eye, black letter fonts all look very similar: dense, thick letters that resemble the hand-written calligraphic forms used by monks before Gutenberg's extraordinary invention. This style was used throughout Western Europe from the twelfth century well into the seventeenth, and in Germany until the twentieth century—which is why black letter is still associated with Germany and looks "Germanic" to the modern eye.

The lowercase letters of this Gothic font are more straightforward than the elaborate uppercase letters. The uppercase letters have curves and flourishes and it's necessary to give them more stitches than other fonts when using them in knitting. Out of context, it is not always easy to discern the difference between an "E" and a "G," or an "F" and an "I" and a "T" in black letter, so the fact that you may be unable to do so in the knitted letter version is a major quality of this elaborate but beautiful style. However, when knitting words or phrases, it is possible to discern the uppercase letters in context.

Knitters can enjoy adding this beautiful and history-soaked typeface to their projects, as in the "Ex Libris" E-reader Cover featured in this chapter (facing page).

"Ex Libris" E-reader Cover

Make this cozy cover instead of using that faux-leather, book-mimicking e-reader case. Meaning "from the books" in Latin, "ex libris" is a fitting epigraph for an e-book as well as a beautiful phrase to showcase in this design, which references the style of medieval illuminated books.

The pattern

Finished size: to fit Kindle Fire e-reader (7½ by 4¾ by ½ in/190 by 120 by 12 mm)
Gauge: 37 sts and 52 rows over 4 in/10 cm in st st on US 0/2 mm needles

Letter motif

If you would like to use different words, use Blackletter Lowercase Charts on pages 136–37. Your chosen words should not exceed 5 or 6 letters per line. You may want to chart out your letters so that they fit together (see how the letters "i" and "s" fit together on the "Ex Libris" Chart on page 89) to save space. Your chosen words should not exceed 58 sts. Be sure to center your words horizontally over the 60 st space inside the leaf border and vertically over the 44 row space, leaving 2 rows between lines.

Front

Using MC and knitting needles, CO 72 sts.
Row 1 (WS): Purl.
Row 2 (RS): Knit.
Row 3: Purl.

Commence "Ex Libris" Chart

Row 1 (RS): K2, work "Ex Libris" Chart, k2.
Row 2 (WS): P2, work "Ex Libris" Chart, p2.
Rep rows 1 and 2 until 52 rows of chart are complete.

With MC only starting a k row, work 3 more rows in st st. ▶

You will need

Yarn

Jamieson's Shetland Spindrift
(2 ply, fingering weight, 100% wool, 115 yd/105 m per 1 oz/25 g)
[MC] Mooskit (shade 304), 2 balls
[CC1] Spagnum (shade 233), 1 ball
[CC2] Admiral Navy (shade 727), 1 ball

Needles

US 0/2 mm knitting needles
US 0/2 mm DPNs
Tapestry needle

Other

Scissors
Stitch marker

BO purlwise.

Back

Using MC and knitting needles, CO 72 sts.

Starting with a p row, work st st for 58 rows, until piece matches front, ending with a k row.

BO purlwise.

Finishing

Weave in ends and block pieces before seaming. To seam, place pieces RS tog. Using backstich, sew three seams leaving one short end of the cover open.

Turn RS out.

Using DPNs and MC, pick up and k approx. 108 sts (you will need an even number of sts) from around the open edge of the cover. Place marker to indicate beg of the rnd. Work in k1, p1 rib for 4 rnds.

BO in rib.

Weave in ends.

"Ex Libris" Chart

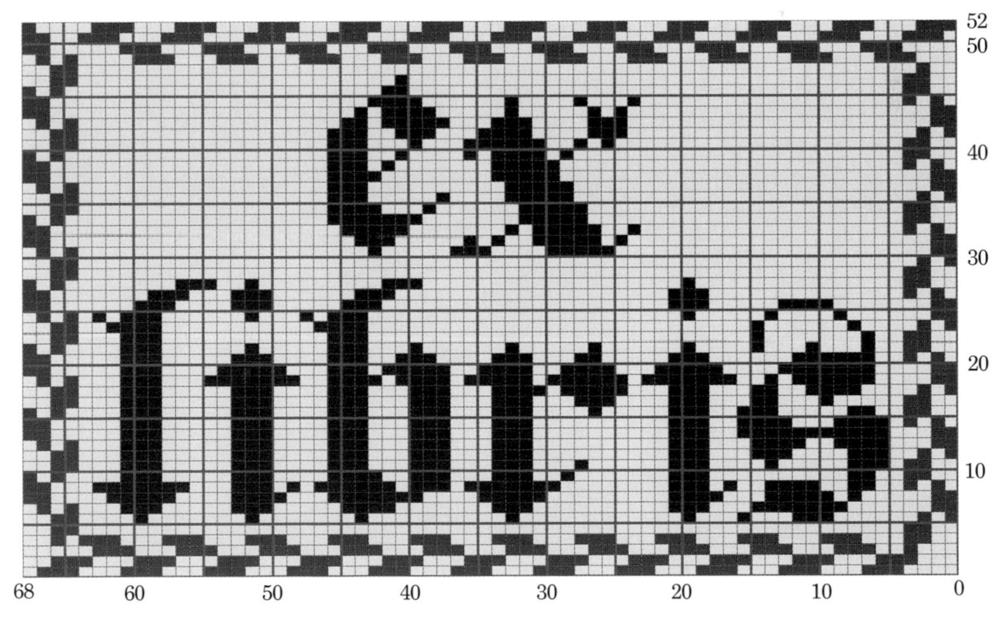

Black Letter Beanie

An ideal way of showing off the bold yet flowing lines of the Black Letter typeface, this initialed Gothic letter hat can be personalized with the wearer's initial or whichever of the letters you're most attracted to.

The pattern

Finished size: To fit average adult head, 20 in/51 cm circumference
Gauge: 17 sts and 20 rows over 4 in/10 cm in st st on US 8/5 mm needles

Letter motif

Use the Letter "D" Chart on the facing page. To substitute your own letter, use the Black Letter Uppercase Charts on pages 133–35. Make sure your chosen letter is centered by working more or fewer sts either side of the letter chart on the body of the hat.

Brim

With MC, CO 66 sts.

Row 1 (RS): (K2, p2) to last 2 sts, k2.
Row 2 (WS): (P2, k2) to last 2 sts, p2.
Rep rows 1 and 2 until piece measures 1 in/2.5 cm from cast-on edge, ending with a RS row.

Next Row (WS): P6, (pfb, p1) to last 6 sts, p6. *93 sts*

Body of hat

Commence Letter "D" Chart

Row 1 (RS): K34, work sts 1 to 25 of Letter "D" Chart, k34.
Row 2 (WS): P34, work sts 1 to 25 of Letter "D" Chart, k34.
(If using a letter that is more or less than 25 sts, such as the letter "M," work more or fewer sts either side of the letter chart so that the letter is centered.)

You will need

Yarn

Bulky BC Garn Semilla Grosso (Bulky)
(100% wool, 87 yd/80 m per 1¾ oz/50 g)
[MC] Gray (shade 101), 2 balls
[CC] Black (shade 02), 1 ball

Needles

US 8/5 mm knitting needles
Tapestry needle

Other

Scissors

Rep prev 2 rows until chart is complete.

Cont with MC only in st st until piece measures 7 in/18 cm from CO edge, ending with a WS row.

Dec for crown

Row 1 (RS): K1, * k5, k2tog; rep from * to last st, k1. *80 sts*
Row 2 and all foll WS rows: Purl.
Row 3: K1, * k4, k2tog; rep from * to last st, k1. *67 sts*
Row 5: K1, * k3, k2tog; rep from * to last st, k1. *54 sts*
Row 7: K1, * k2, k2tog; rep from * to last st, k1. *41 sts*
Row 9: K1, * k1, k2tog; rep from * to last st, k1. *28 sts*
Row 11: K1, (k2tog) to last st, k1. *15 sts*
Row 13: (K1, k2tog) to end. *10 sts*

Finishing

Break yarn, thread through rem 10 sts, and draw tog tightly. Sew the edges of the hat tog using mattress st and weave in ends on the inside of the hat.

Letter "D" Chart

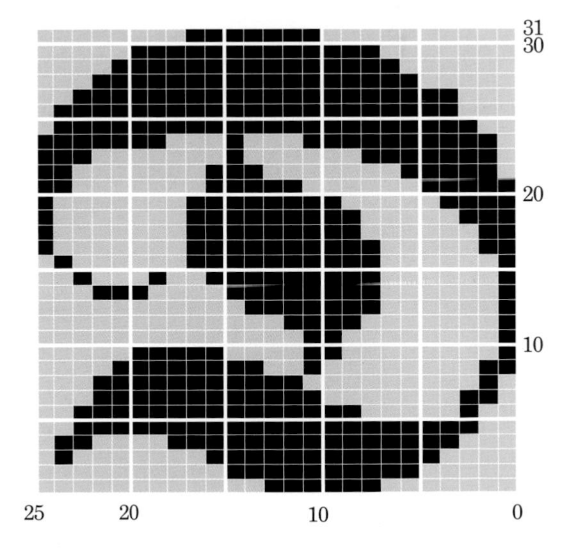

"Carpe Diem" Covered Bracelets

Seize the day with these chunky knit-covered bracelets, which are modeled after tattoos but won't hurt your wrists nearly as much.

The pattern

Finished size: approx. 11½ in/29 cm circumference by 2¾ in/7 cm wide

Gauge: Approx. 25 sts and 35 rows over 4 in/10 cm in st st on US 3/3.25 mm needles

Letter motif

Use the "Carpe" and "Diem" Charts on facing page. If you are changing the wording, use the Black Letter Lowercase Charts on pages 136–37. You will be able to fit a maximum of 5 letters. Draw a box 1 st wider than your chosen letters; this will show you the amount of space you have between each letter. Make sure the smaller letters start at row 8 and finish on row 25. Longer letters will start below or above these rows.

"Carpe" bracelet

Using MC, CO 72 sts.

Starting with a k row, work 3 rows in st st.

BO.

Commence "Carpe" Chart

Using the intarsia technique and CC as indicated, work rows 1–28 of chart.

Using MC only, work 7 rows in st st.

BO.

You will need

Yarn

Rowan Felted Tweed DK (50% merino wool/ 25% alpaca/25% viscose; 191 yd/175 m per 1¾ oz/50 g)
[MC] Clay (shade 177), 1 ball
[CC] Carbon (shade 159), 1 ball

Needles

US 3/3.25 mm knitting needles
Tapestry needle

Other

Scissors
2 chunky bracelets, approx. 11½ in/29 cm around outside of bracelet, 2¾ in/7 cm deep from top to bottom
Safety pins

"Diem" bracelet

Using MC, CO 72 sts.

Starting with a k row, work 8 rows in st st.

BO.

Commence "Diem" Chart

Using the intarsia technique and CC as indicated, work rows 1–23 of chart.

Using MC only, work 5 rows in st st.

BO.

Finishing

Block or press fabric to finished size following the ball band instructions and sew side seams tog to make a ring. Sl bracelet into the knitting with the RSF. Wrap the fabric around the bracelet—use safety pins to hold the seam tog. Seam up the bound-off and cast-on edges to completely enclose the bracelet.

"Carpe" Chart

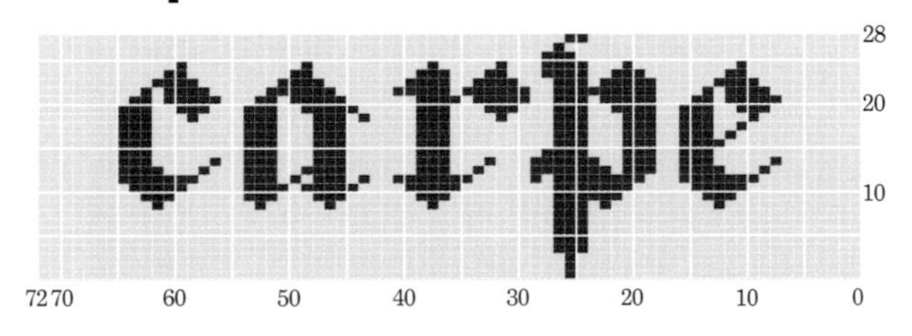

"Diem" Chart

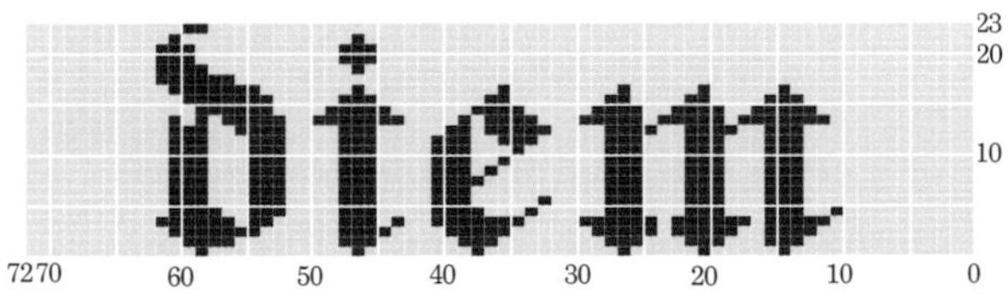

8 Numbers and Punctuation

You may be surprised to learn that using punctuation symbols to form "emoticons" did not originate with the Internet or instant messaging. In fact, the use of emoticons in writing has been traced back to the eighteenth century, and some forms were in wide usage by the nineteenth century.

Of course, the age of the Internet, Web forums, instant messaging, and online gaming has seen a meteoric rise in the use of these symbols. But punctuation can be beautiful even out of context: For example, the sweeping curves of an ampersand (&) or the exclamatory and dramatic question mark (?) and exclamation point (!). With the omnipresence of email and Twitter helping the process, the "at" symbol (@) has enjoyed newfound popularity, and all these symbols and more are included in the charts on pages 138–39 for you to create fun designs with.

Including number charts in this book means knitters can incorporate special dates, times, street addresses, lucky numbers, sports jersey numbers, or even longitude and latitude coordinates into their knitting. The Wedding Pillow project in this chapter (facing page) will give you an idea of what's possible.

Monaco, the typeface on which these charts are based, has simple, almost childlike clean lines, to aid in readability and clarity. These symbols and numbers will make a clean, bold statement in your own projects.

Wedding Pillow

This lovingly knitted pillow to bear the wedding rings is the perfect contribution to the happy couple's big day, as well as a lovely memento to be enjoyed for years to come.

The pattern

Finished size: approx. 10 in/25 cm square
Gauge: 28 sts and 36 rows over 4 in/10 cm in st st on US 2/3 mm knitting needles.

Letter motif

Using the Wedding Pillow Chart (page 97) as an example, use the Script Uppercase Charts on pages 120–23 for the initials. On the chart of your chosen letter, draw a box around the letter that fits exactly the width and height of your chosen letters. Use the Numbers and Punctuation Charts on pages 138–39 for the date. On the chart of your chosen numbers, draw a box around each of the numbers that fits exactly the width and height of your chosen numbers.

The patt on the pillow is added after the main fabric has been worked using duplicate stitch (see page 23).

Front and back panels

Using MC, CO 70 sts.

Starting with a k row, work in st st for 90 rows.

BO.

Rep for back panel to match front. ▶

You will need

Yarn

Rowan Cotton Glacé (sportweight, 100% cotton, 125 yd/115 m per 1¾ oz/50 g)
[MC] Ecru (shade 725), 2 balls
[CC] Black (shade 727), 1 ball

Needles

US 2/3 mm knitting needles
Tapestry needle

Other

Scissors
Square pillow form, 10 in/25 cm
Sewing needle and thread

6.9.14

Duplicate Stitch Chart

Using the chart (below) as a guide and using duplicate stitch, apply the date and initials to the front panel of the pillow.

Finishing

Weave in ends and block or press to finished dimensions following directions on the ball band. Sew front and back panels together at the bound-off and cast-on edge, leaving open one of the side seams. Insert the pillow form and close rem seam.

Wedding Pillow Chart

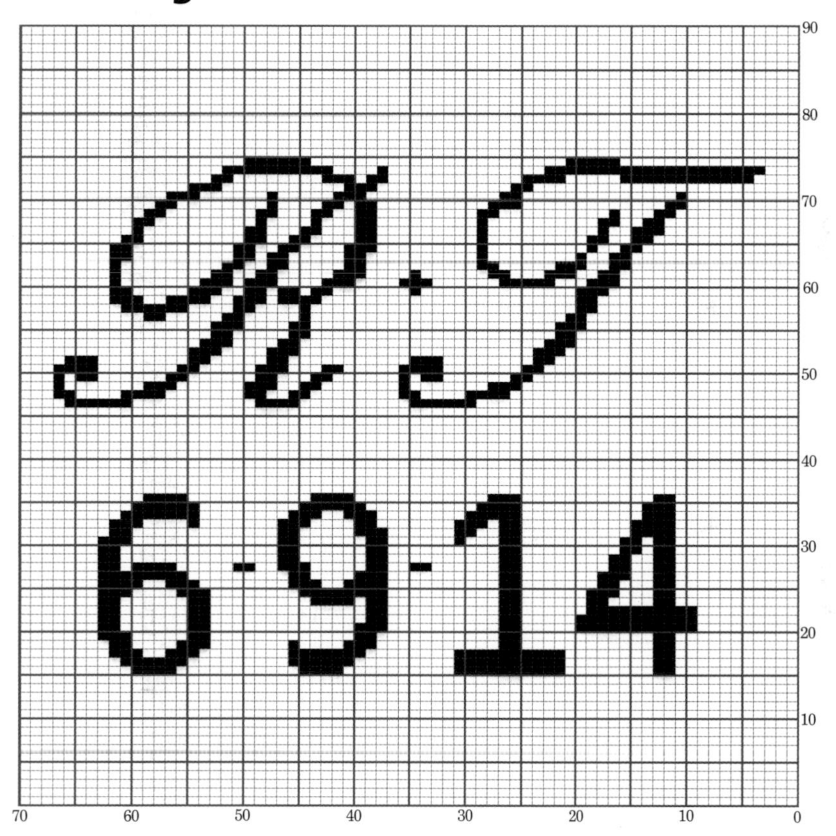

9 3-D LETTERS

Although the projects in this chapter do not adhere to a specific typeface group or font (other than generally being sans serif), they were a must in a book about knitted letters. The letters here are redolent of fanciful, cartoony bubble letter writing. Bubble letter fonts have been designed for decades as novelty computer fonts, but of course everyone remembers hand-drawing these lovable letters as children.

The A–Z Bookends (facing page) are a wonderful gift idea for someone with a love of literature and a lot of books that need to be attractively propped up. The "LOVE" 3-D Letter Pillows (page 103) are a great way to practice new stitch patterns as well as shaping.

When making 3-D letters, careful shaping is used to promote readability and to ensure that the piece will hold its shape when stuffed. Be sure to stuff firmly, but not so much that the stitches stretch. When stuffing, use small pieces one at a time to prevent lumps, and use a firm stitch gauge for structure and ease of filling.

A–Z Bookends

However you organize your personal library—alphabetically, by subject, or by spine color if you're a real aesthete—any book collection will benefit from being propped up by these beautiful, sturdy knitted bookends.

The patterns

Finished size: approx. 10 in/25 cm by 9 in/22.5 cm
Gauge: 16 sts and 23 rows over 4 in/10 cm in garter st on US 8/5 mm needles

Both projects are knitted in garter stitch (all rows k).

Letter "A"

CO 13 sts and work 13 rows in garter st.

Break yarn and sl sts to holder.

CO a second set of 13 sts and work 13 rows in garter st.

Row 14 (WS): K13, CO 13 sts, slip 13 sts from holder to working needle and k to end. *39 sts*
Rows 15–26: Knit.
Row 27 (RS): K13, BO 13 sts, K13 with a separate ball of yarn. Cont working both sides of the letter separately.
Row 28 (WS): K2tog, k12, M1 on first side. M1, k12, K2tog on second side. *13 sts on each side*
Row 29 (RS): Knit.
Rows 30–39: Rep last two rows 5 times.
Row 40 (WS): Work across all sts to join top of letter. K12, k2tog, k12. *25 sts*
Row 41 (RS): Knit.
Row 42 (WS): K2tog, k to last 2 sts, k2tog. *23sts*
Rep last two rows until 13 sts remain.

BO. ▶

You will need

Yarn
Rowan Felted Tweed (Aran) (50% wool/ 25% alpaca/25% viscose, approx. 95 yd/ 87 m per 1¾ oz/50 g ball)
For "A": Ivy (shade 727), 2 balls
For "Z": Cherry (shade 732), 2 balls

Needles
US 8/5 mm knitting needles
Tapestry needle

Other
Scissors
Stitch holder
Plastic canvas sheeting, about 20 in/50 cm square
Lightweight polyester toy stuffing
Dried beans, 35 oz/1 kg

HORSES & PONIES
SEA & SEASHORE
ANCIENT & ROMAN BRITAIN
SEASHELLS
HORSES & PONIES
CACTI
SHIPS
TREES
WILD ANIMALS
WEATHER
MUSIC
PURE STYLE
PETER OBORNE
THE TRIUMPH OF THE POLITICAL CLASS

Rep all of this for the back side of the letter. When working across the entire width of the letter, only one thread of yarn is required.

Depth creation and finishing

Measure and cut 2 pieces of plastic canvas to fit inside the letter. St the canvas to the rev sides of the front and back pieces at several points to prevent slipping and to provide stability and shape definition for the bookends.

CO 15 sts and work in garter stitch until work is long enough to fit around the inner triangle of the "A" (approx. 7 in/18 cm). Keep measuring and checking the length and BO when it is long enough. St in place using mattress st to secure the front of the "A" to the back.

CO 15 sts and work in garter stitch until the work is long enough to reach the entire outside length of the letter (approx. 30 in/76 cm). Keep measuring and checking the length and BO when it is long enough. St in place using mattress stitch, leaving sufficient gaps for the dried beans to be added to the base of the letter. Fill the top half of the letter with lightweight polyester toy stuffing and st up to complete.

Letter "Z"

CO 39 sts and work 14 rows in garter st.

Row 15: BO 20 sts, k to last 2 sts, skpo. *18 sts*
Row 16: K2tog, k to end. *17 sts*
Row 17: M1, k to last 2 sts, skpo.
Row 18: As row 16. *16 sts*
Row 19: As row 17.
Row 20: K2tog, k to last st, m1 in last st.
Row 21: As row 17.
Row 22: As row 20.
Row 23: As row 17.
Row 24: Knit.
Row 25: As row 17.
Row 26: As row 20. ▶

"A" Bookend Chart

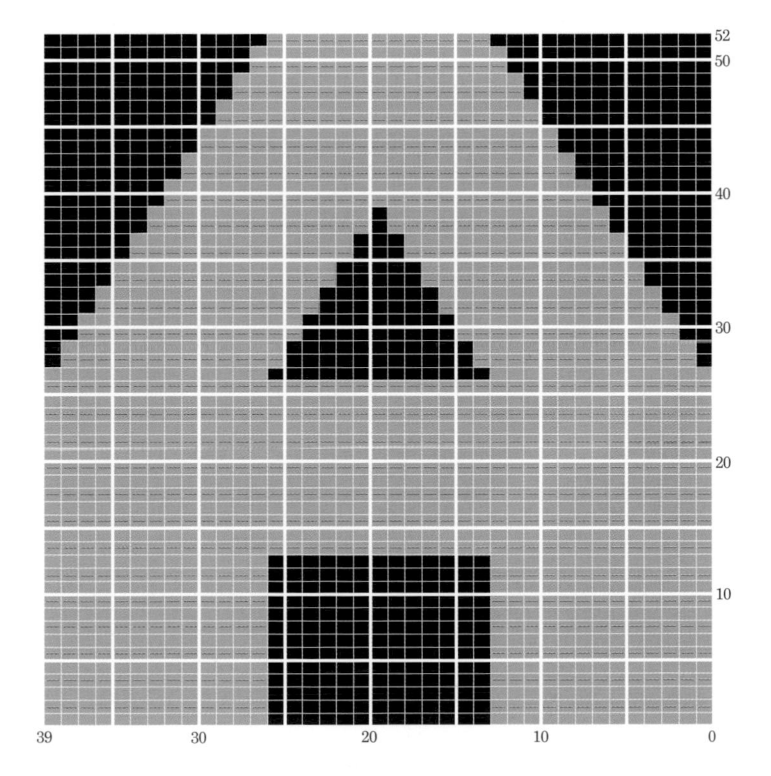

Row 27: As row 17.
Row 28: As row 20.
Row 29: As row 17.
Row 30: As row 24.
Row 31: As row 17.
Row 32: As row 20.
Row 33: As row 17.
Row 34: As row 20.
Row 35: As row 17.
Row 36: As row 20.
Row 37: M1, k to end. *17 sts*
Row 38: As row 20.
Row 39: M1, k to end. *18 sts*
Row 40: As row 16. *17 sts*
Row 41: K to end, CO 22 sts. *39 sts*
Rows 42–50: Knit.

BO.

Rep all of this for the back side of the letter—because this is created using garter stitch, it is not necessary to reverse the instructions.

Depth creation and making up

Measure and cut out 2 pieces of plastic canvas to fit inside the "Z." St the canvas to the reverse sides of the front and back pieces at several points to prevent slipping and to provide stability and shape definition for the bookends.

CO 17 sts. Work in garter stitch until work is long enough to fit around the outside of letter Z (approx 42 in/107 cm). Keep measuring and checking the length and BO when it is long enough. St in place using mattress stitch, leaving sufficient gaps for the dried beans to be added to the base of the letter. Fill the top half of the letter with lightweight polyester toy stuffing and st up to complete.

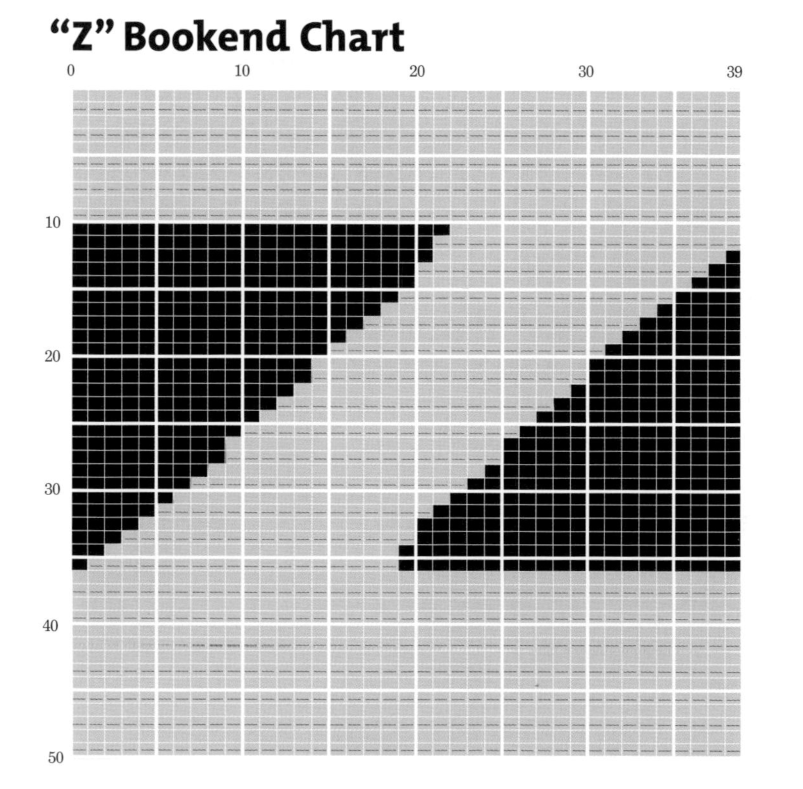

"LOVE" 3-D Letter Pillows

These chunky, comfy pillows will cozy up any spot in the house, from a kitchen ledge to a warm sofa.

The patterns

Gauge (all four letters): 13 sts and 18 rows over 4 in/ 10 cm on US 101/6.5 mm needles

Note: You need to make two sides for each pillow, which means that the back side is the letter in reverse. This is referred to in the patt as the "reverse" side, as opposed to the "front" side.

You will need

Yarn

Rowan Purelife British Sheep Breeds Undyed (100% wool, 120 yd/110 m per 3½ oz/100 g)
Masham (shade 957), 1 ball per pillow

Needles

US 101/6.5 mm knitting needles

Other

Scissors
Large bag of polyester toy stuffing

"L" Pillow

This letter is made using a wide rib, giving definition to the long side of the letter.

Finished size: 12 in/30 cm by 12 in/30 cm

Front side

CO 41 sts.

Row 1 (RS): K2, p1, * k4, p1; rep from * to last 3 sts, k3.
Row 2 (WS): P3, * k1, p4; rep from * to last 2 sts, k2.
Rep rows 1 and 2 a further eight times.

Row 19: BO 31 sts, k2, p1, * k4, p1; rep from * last 3 sts, k3.
Row 20: P3, * k1, p4; rep from * to last 2 sts, k2.
Rep rows 19 and 20 a further fourteen times.

BO knitwise.

Reverse side

CO 41 sts.
Row 1 (RS): K3, p1, * k4, p1; rep from * to last 2 sts, k2.
Row 2 (WS): P2, * k1, p4; rep from * to last 3 sts, k3. ▶

Rep rows 1 and 2 a further eight times and then row 1 once more.

Row 20 (WS): BO 31 sts, k2, p1, * k4, p1; rep from * to last 3 sts, k3.
Row 21: P3, * k1, p4; rep from * to last 2 sts, k2.
Rep rows 20 and 21 a further thirteen times.

BO knitwise.

See "Finishing for all letters," page 107.

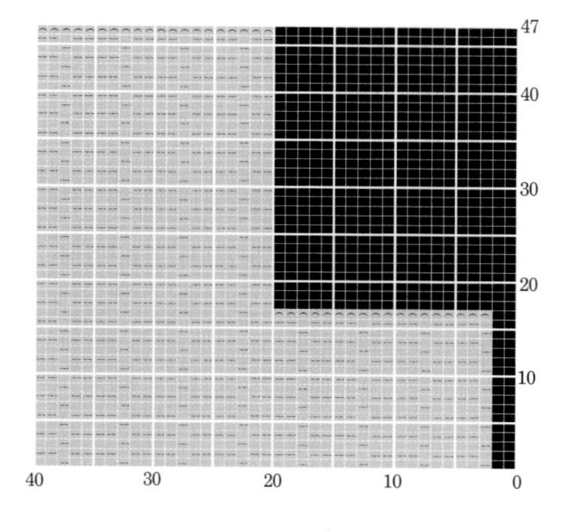

"O" Pillow

This letter is made using seed st, giving a textured patt to the letter.
Finished size: 12 in/30 cm by 12 in/30 cm

Front and reverse sides

CO 13 sts.

Row 1 (RS): * K1, p1; rep from * to end. *13 sts*
Row 2 (WS): K1f&b, * k1, p1; rep from * to last st, k1f&b. *2 sts inc*
Row 3: K1f&b, * p1, k1; rep from * to last st, k1f&b. *2 sts inc*
Rows 4–14: Rep rows 2 and 3 until you have 39 sts on the needles.
Row 15: * P1, k1; rep from * to end.
Rows 16–19: As row 15.
Row 20: (P1, k1) eight times. BO 3 sts. * P1, k1; rep from * to end. *36 sts* ▶

TYPHOON

Row 21: (P1, k1) seven times. P1, k2tog join new ball of yarn to other side of bound-off sts and cont row 21 in reverse as follows: K2tog, p1, (k1, p1) to end.
Row 22: (P1, k1) seven times, p1, k2tog, cont row 22 in rev as follows: P1, (k1, p1) to end.
Rows 22–29: As row 22.
Row 30: (P1, k1) seven times, p1, k2tog, cont row 30 in rev as follows: K2tog, p1, (k1, p1) to end.
Row 31: (P1, k1) eight times. CO 3 sts. (P1, k1) to end.
Rows 32–37: (P1, k1) to end.
Row 38: K2tog, * p1, k1; rep to last 2 sts. K2tog.
Rows 39–50: Rep row 38 until 13 sts rem.

BO knitwise.

See "Finishing for all letters," facing page.

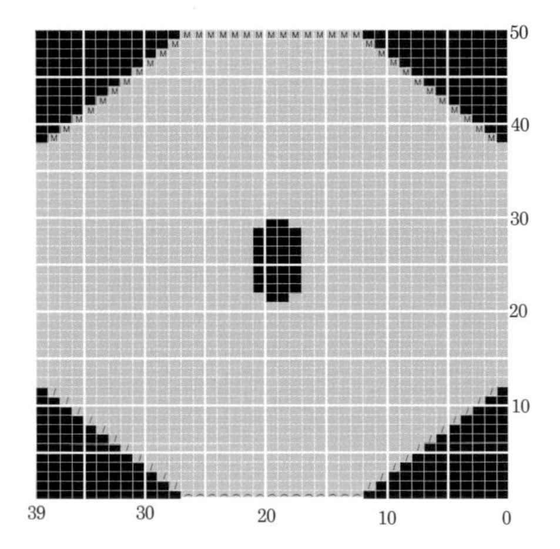

"V" Pillow

This letter is made using a rib-like patt, with a guiding row of p sts to emphasize the "V" shape.

Finished size: 10 in/25 cm by 12 in/30 cm

Front and reverse sides

CO 7 sts.
Row 1 (RS): K2, p1, k1, p1, k2.
Row 2: Inc1, k3, p1, k3, inc1. *9 sts*
Row 3: Inc1, k3, p1, k1, p1, k3, inc1. *11 sts*
Row 4: Inc1, k5, p1, k5, inc1. *13 sts*
Row 5: Inc1, k5, p1, k1, p1, k5, inc1. *15 sts*
Row 6: Inc1, k7, p1, k7, inc1. *17 sts*
Row 7: Inc1, k7, p1, k1, p1, k7, inc1. *19 sts*
Row 8: Inc1, k9, p1, k9, inc1. *21 sts*
Row 9: Inc1, k8, p2, k1, p2, k8, inc1. *23 sts*
Row 10: Inc1, k8, p, k2, p1, k2, p1, k8, inc1. *25 sts*
Row 11: Inc1, k8, p1, k2, p1, k1, p1, k2, p1, k8, inc1. *27 sts*
Row 12: Inc1, k8, p1, k4, p1, k4, p1, k8, inc1. *29 sts*
Row 13: Inc1, k8, p1, k4, p1, k1, p1, k4, p1, k8, inc1. *31 sts*
Row 14: Inc1, k8, p1, k6, p1, k6, p1, k8, inc1. *33 sts*
Row 15: Inc1, k8, p1, k6, p1, k1, p1, k6, p1, k8, inc1. *35 sts*
Row 16: Inc1, k8, p1, k8, p1, k8, p1, k8, inc1. *37 sts*
Row 17: Inc1, k8, p1, k8, p1, k1, p1, k8, p1, k9, inc1. *39 sts*
Row 18: K9, p, k9, p1, k9, p, k9.
Row 19: K9, p, k8, p, k, p, k8, p, k9.
Row 20: K9, p, k9, p1, k9, p, k9.
Split for two limbs of the "V":
Row 21: K9, p1, k9, BO 1 st, k9, p1, k9.
Row 22: K9, p1, k9, cont other limb with separate ball of yarn as follows: K9, p1, k9.
Row 23: K9, p1, k9, cont other limb with separate ball of yarn as follows: K9, p1, k9.
Rows 24–50: Rep rows 22 and 23.

BO knitwise.

See "Finishing for all letters," facing page.

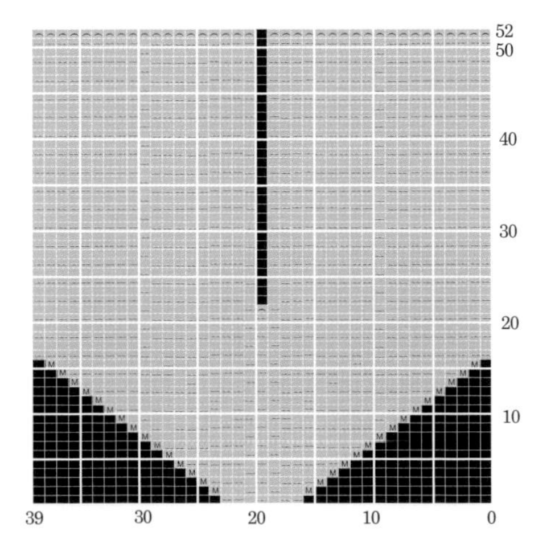

"E" Pillow

This letter is made using basket weave patt.

Finished size: 12 in/30 cm by 10 in/25 cm

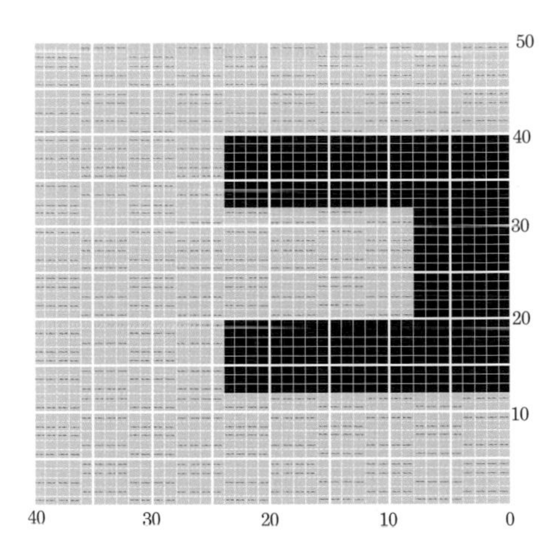

Front side

CO 40 sts
Row 1 (RS): (K4, p4) to end.
Row 2 (WS): (P4, k4) to end.
Row 3: As row 1.
Rows 4–5: As row 2.
Row 6: As row 1.
Row 7: As row 2.
Row 8: As row 1.
These 8 rows form the basket weave patt.
** Rep rows 1–4 once more.
Row 13: BO 24 sts, work in basket weave patt (as row 5) to end. *16 sts*
Row 14: As row 6.
Rep rows 7 and 8, and then rows 1 to 4 once more.
Row 21: Rep row 5, CO 16 sts. *32 sts*
Rows 22–32: Work in basket weave patt.
Row 33: BO 16 sts, work in basket weave patt to end. *16 sts*
Rows 34–37: Cont in basket weave patt, CO 24 sts. *40 sts*

Cont in basket weave patt for a further 15 rows.

BO knitwise.

Reverse side

CO 40 sts.
Row 1 (RS): (P4, k4) to end.
Row 2 (WS): (K4, p4) to end.
Rows 3–4: Rep rows 1 and 2.
Row 5: As row 2.
Rows 6–7: Rep rows 1 and 2.
Row 8: As row 1.
These 8 rows form the reverse basket weave patt.

Work as for front from ** to BO.

Finishing for all letters

Place front and reverse letters wrong sides together and use sl st to join all edges, leaving one side open to allow room for stuffing. Stuff fairly firmly with toy stuffing, ensuring that it is evenly spread through the pillow. Stitch up the final edge, tucking all loose ends inside neatly.

COLORWORK CHARTS

Sans Serif Uppercase Charts

(adapted from Helvetica typeface)

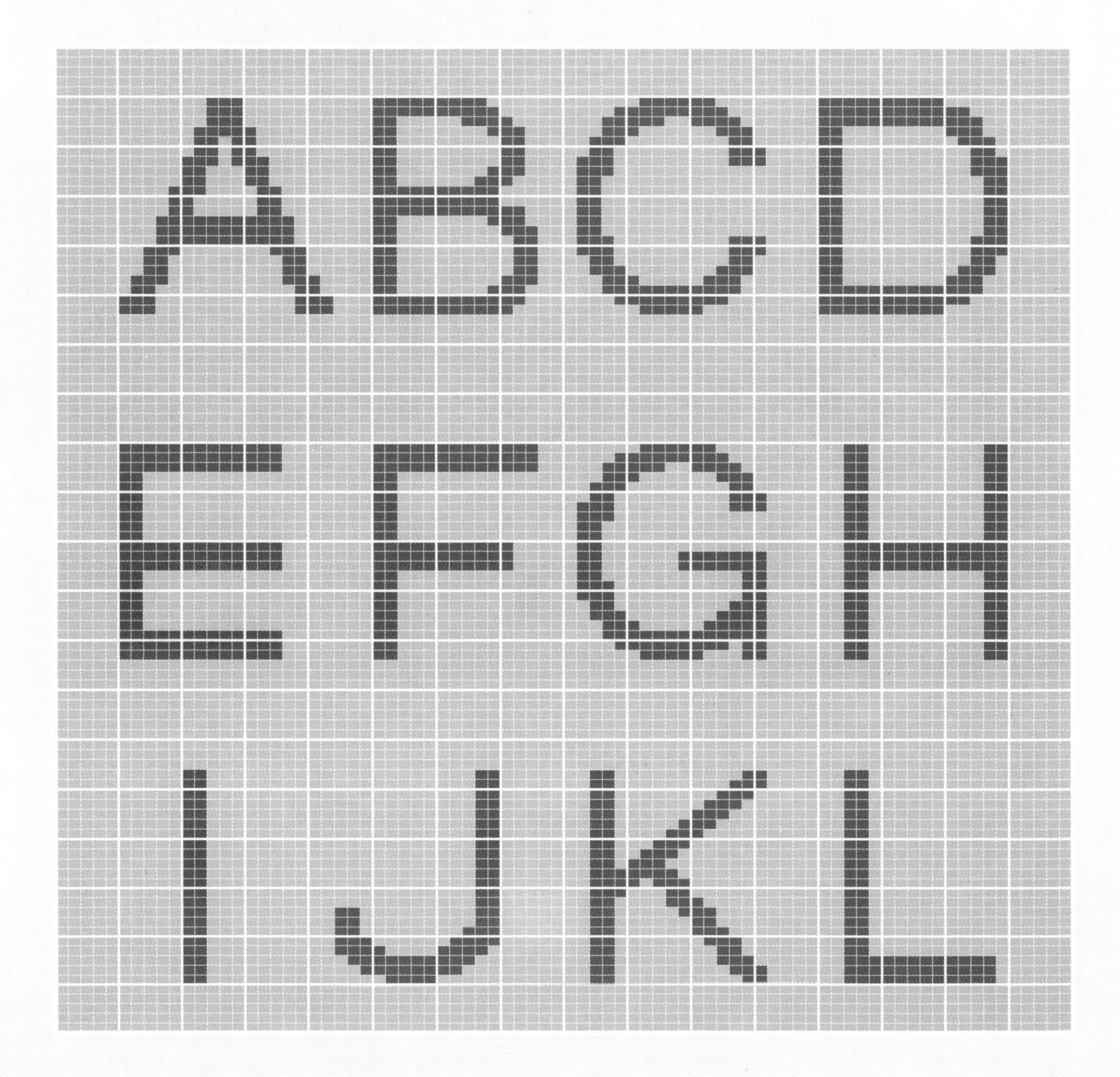

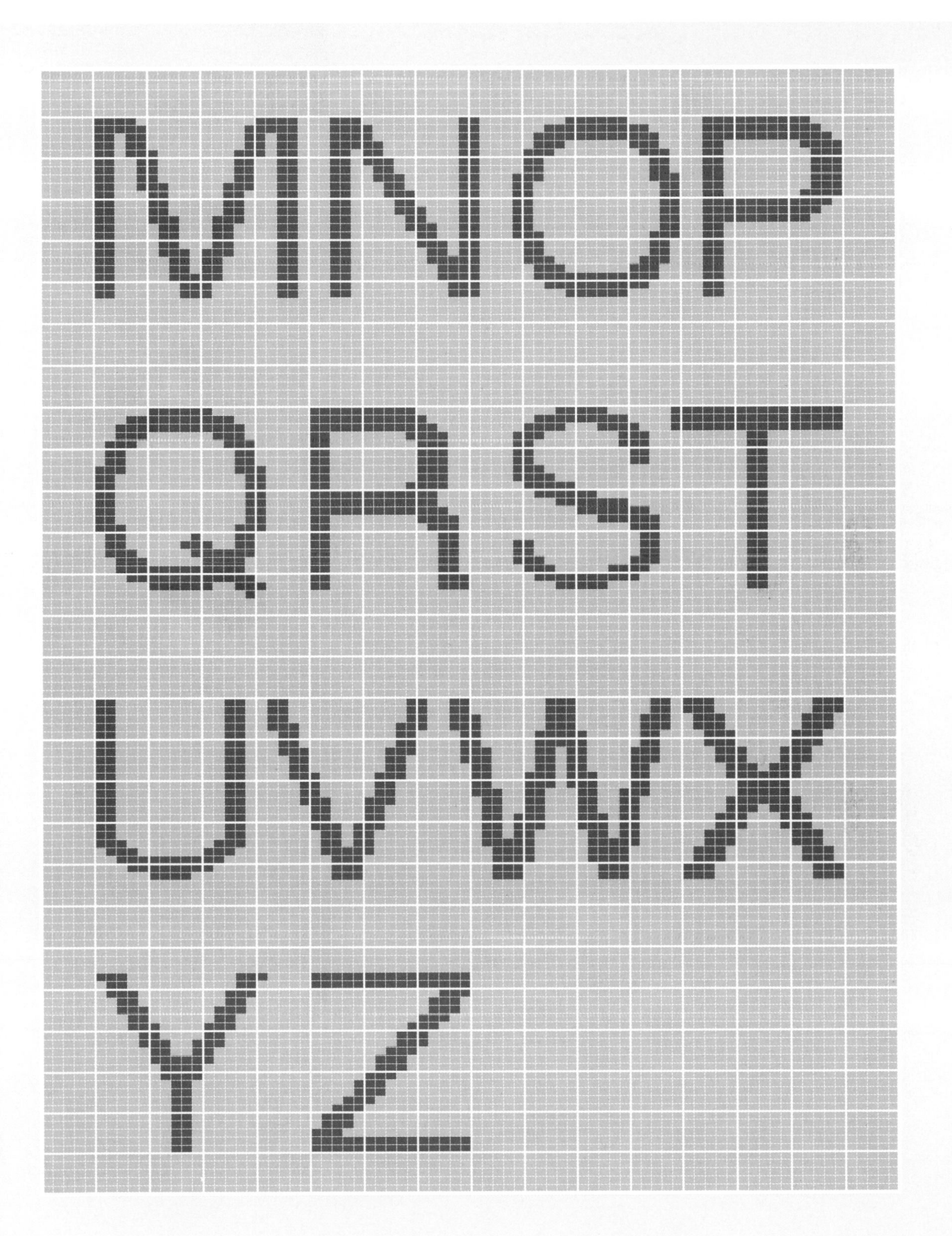

Sans Serif Lowercase Charts

(adapted from Helvetica typeface)

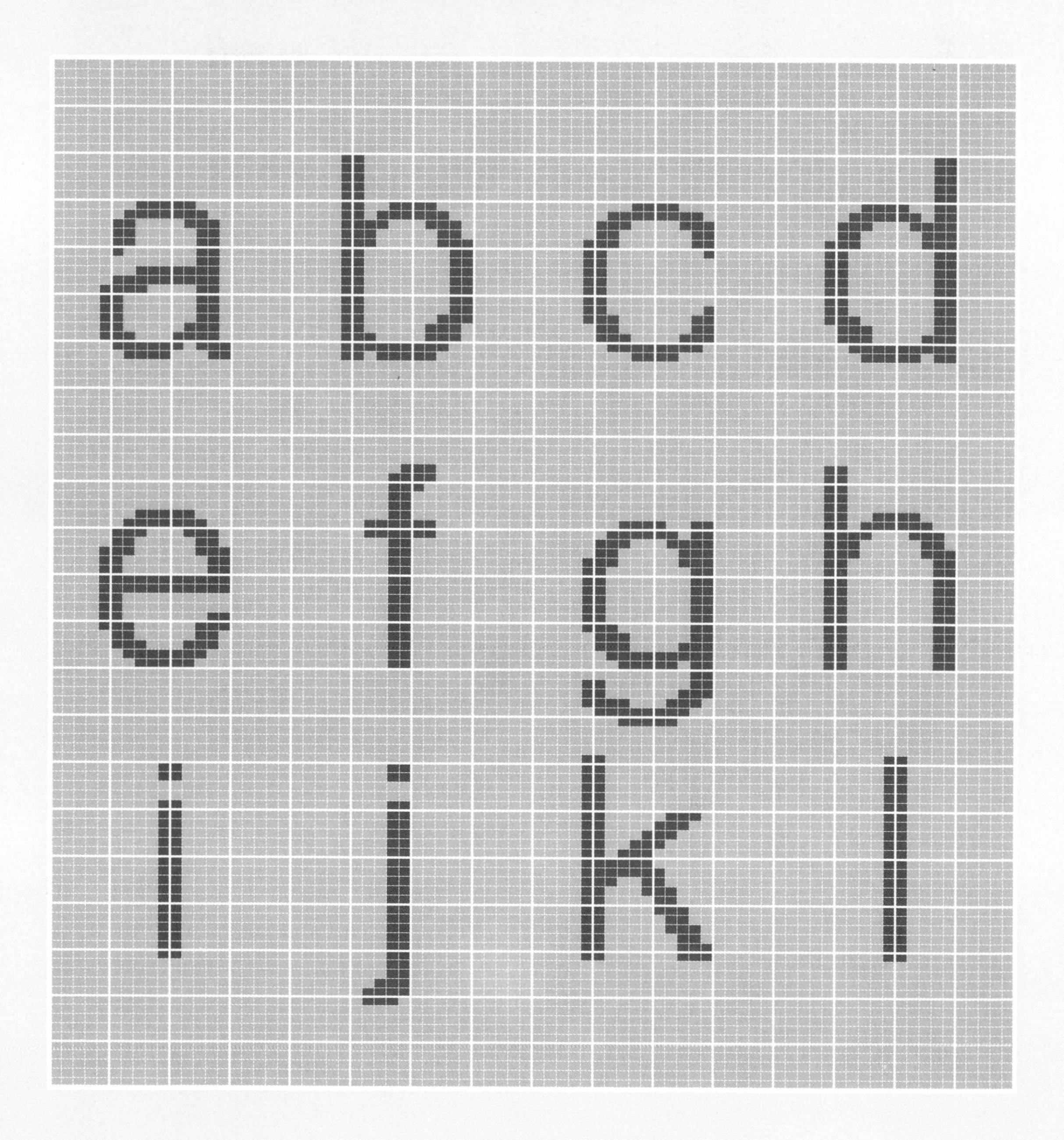

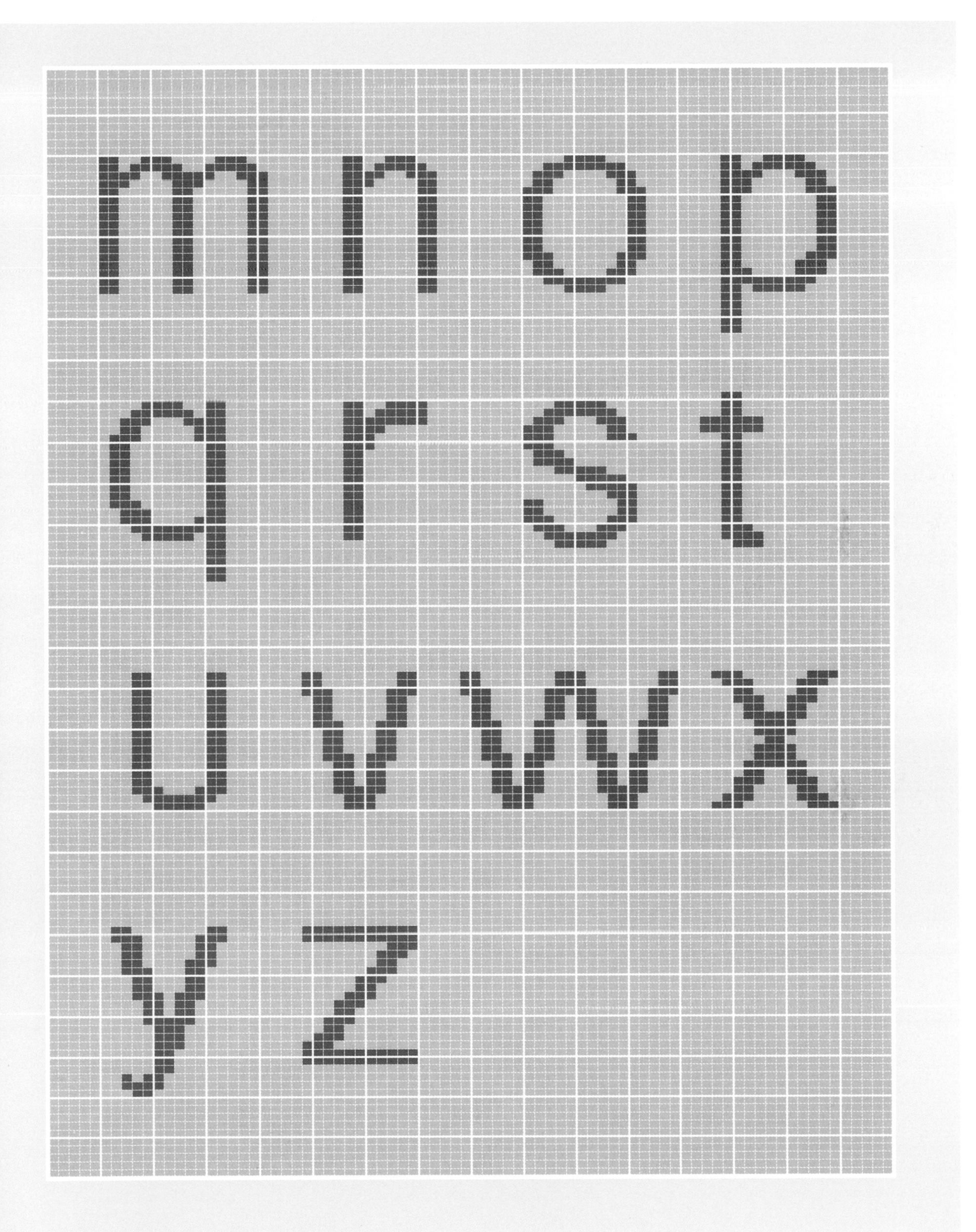

Serif Uppercase Charts

(adapted from Garamond typeface)

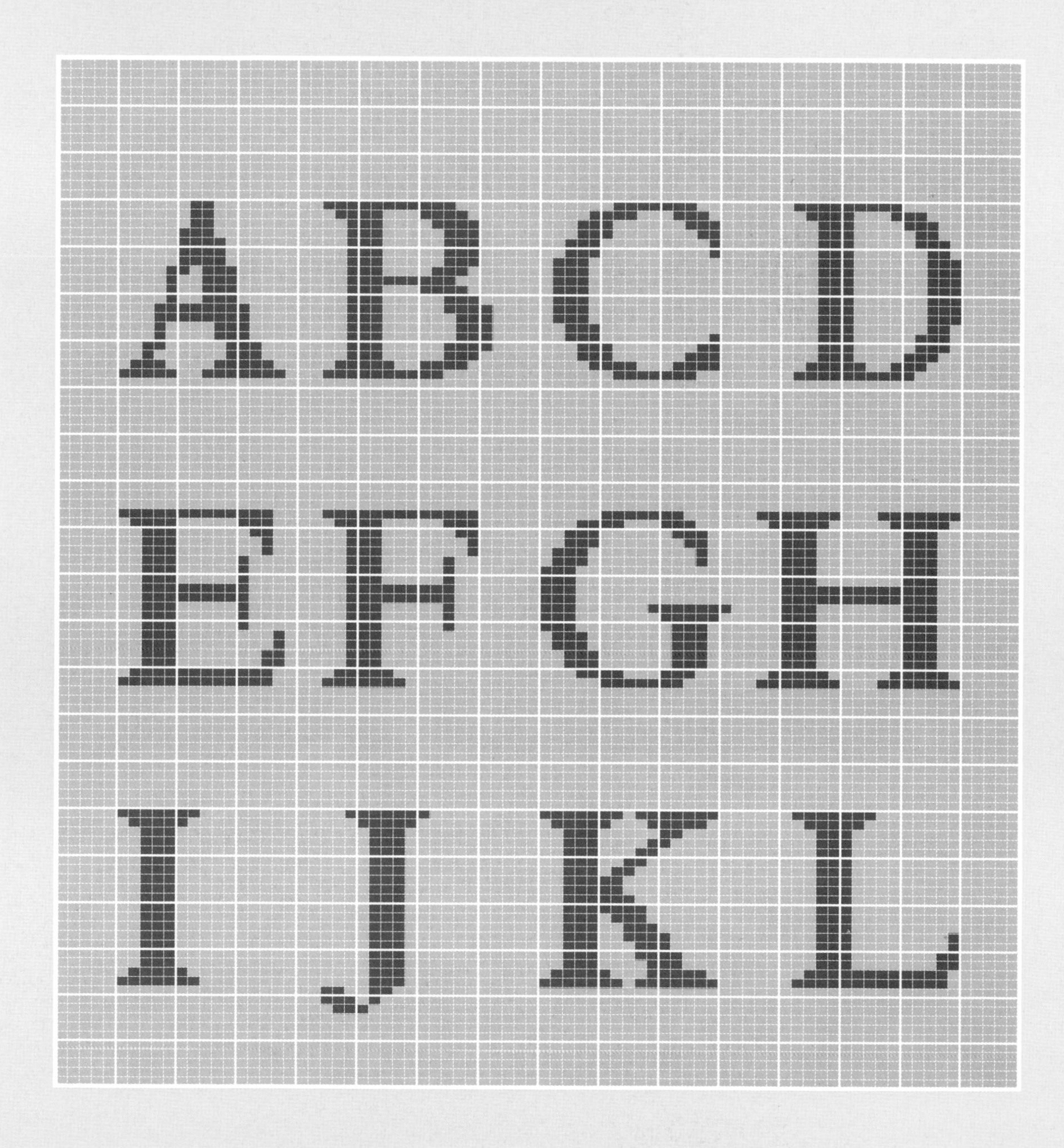

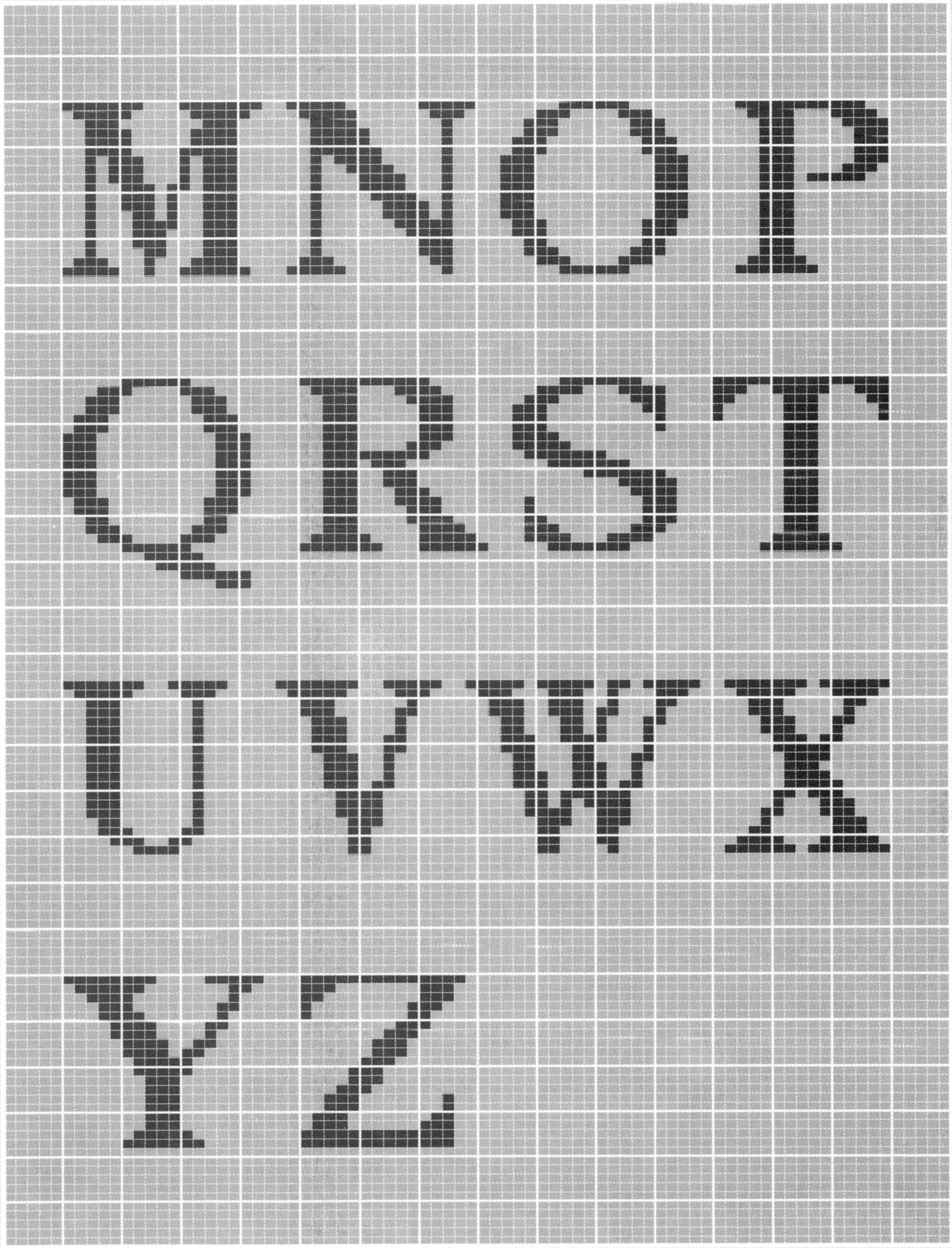

Serif Lowercase Charts

(adapted from Garamond typeface)

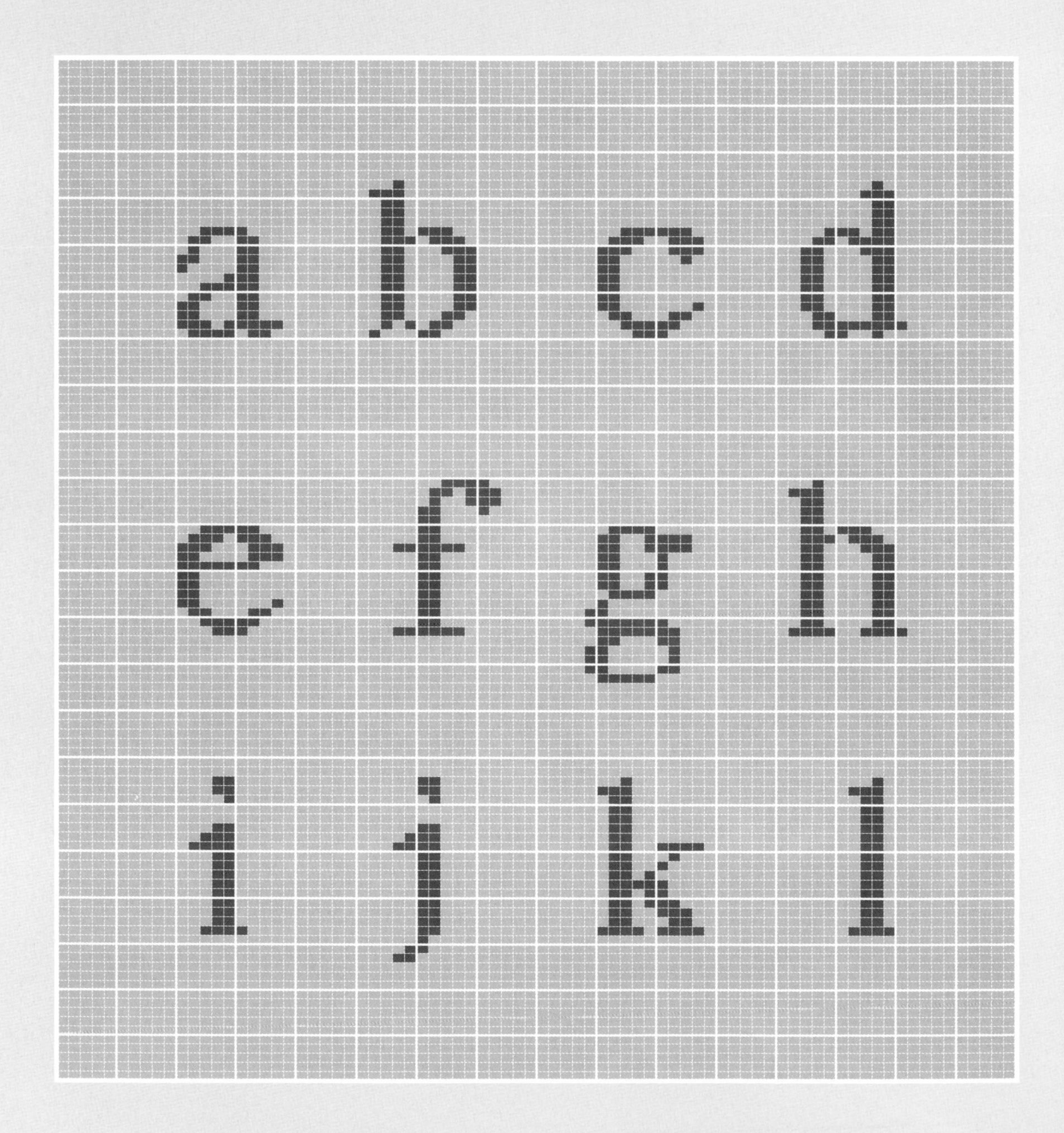

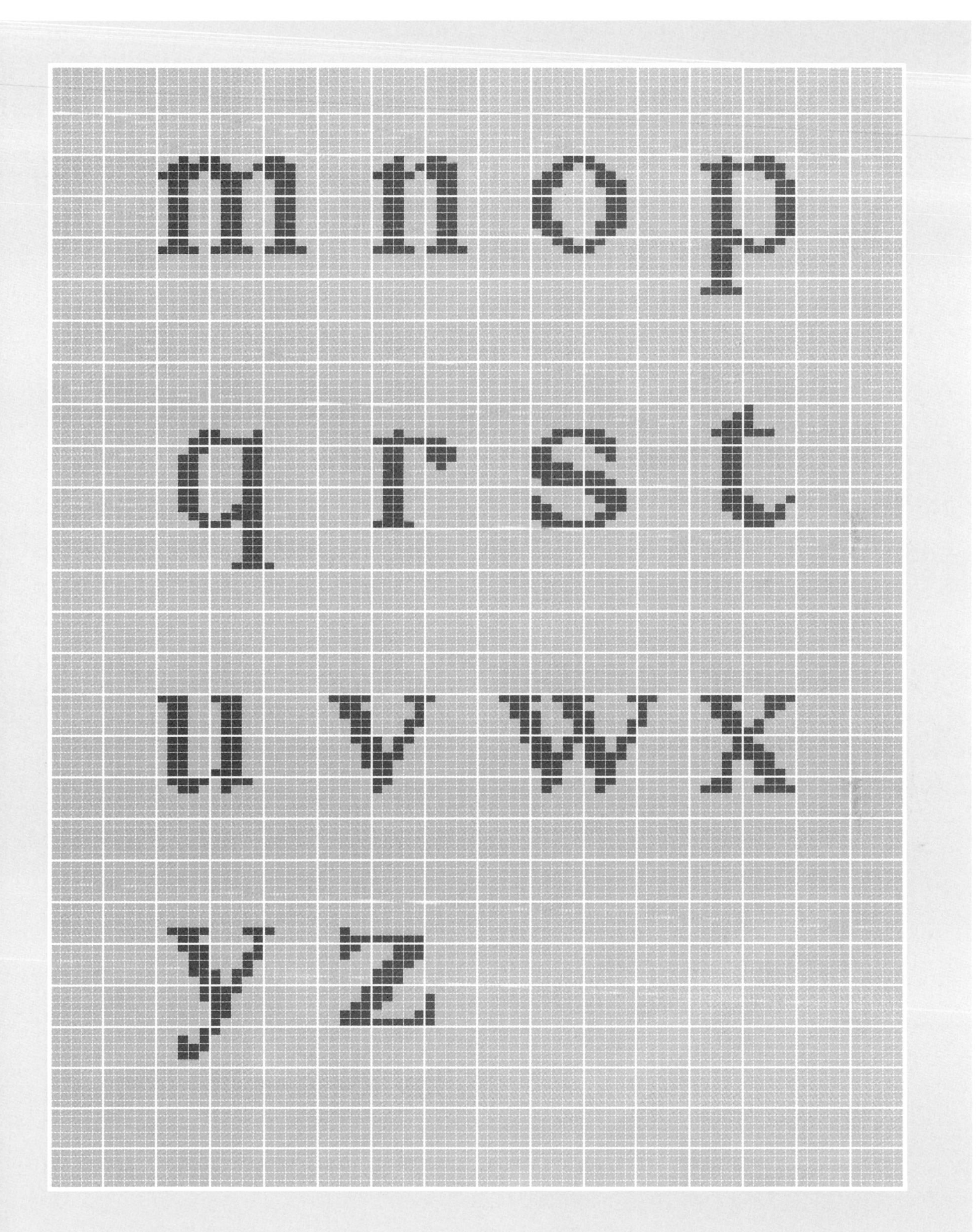
m n o p
q r s t
u v w x
y z

Slab Serif Charts

(adapted from College Slab typeface)

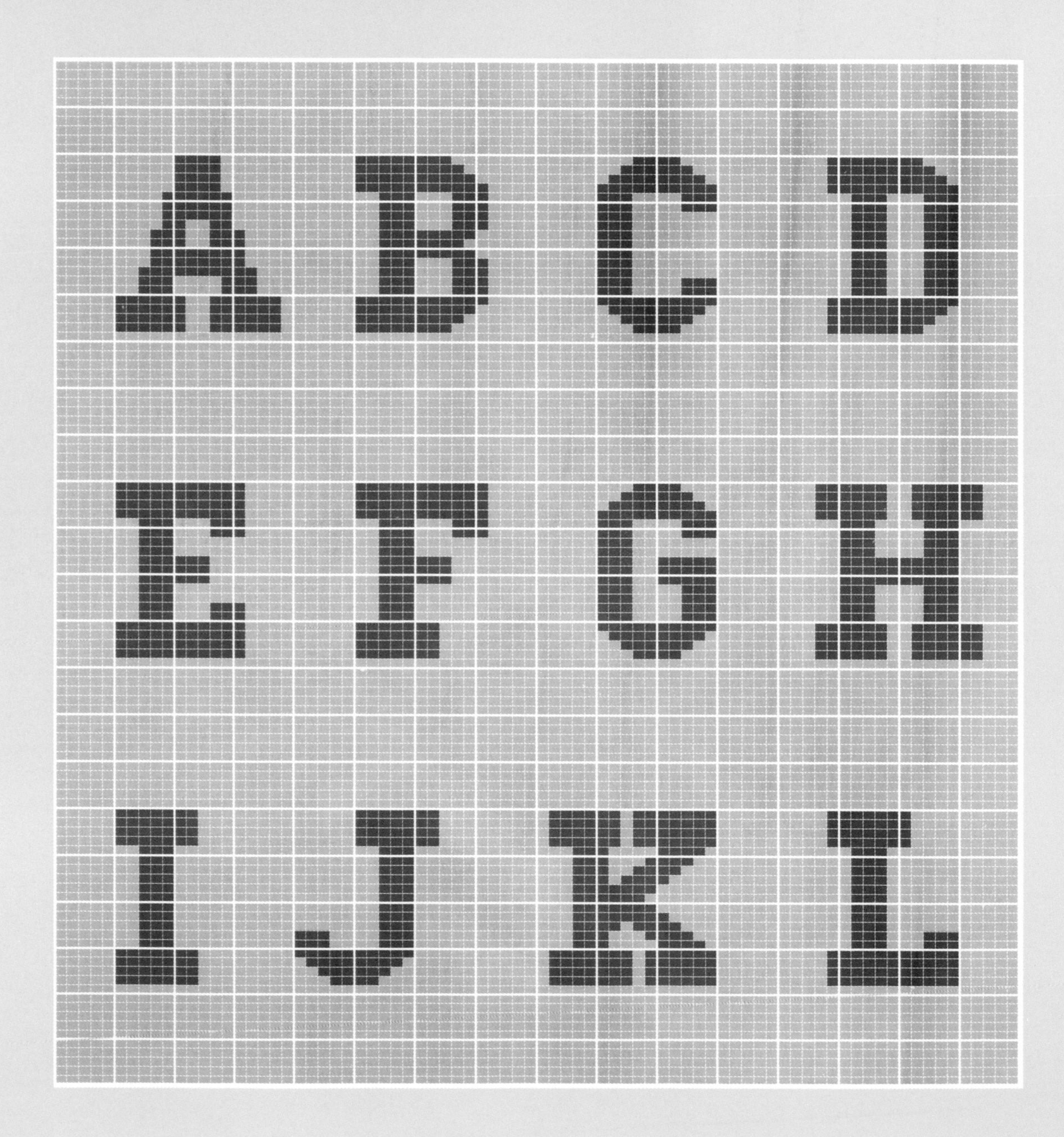

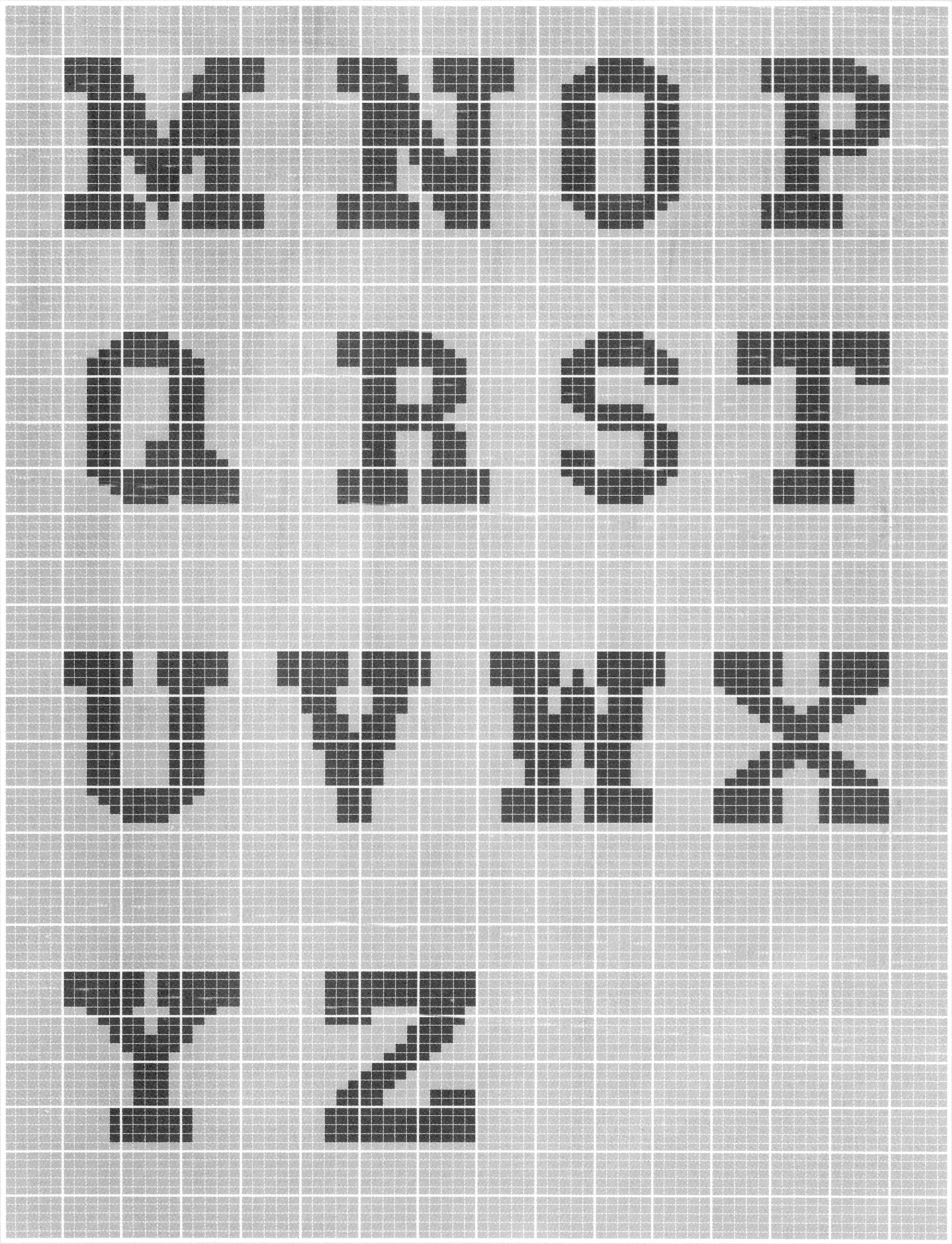

Stencil Charts

(adapted from Stencil typeface)

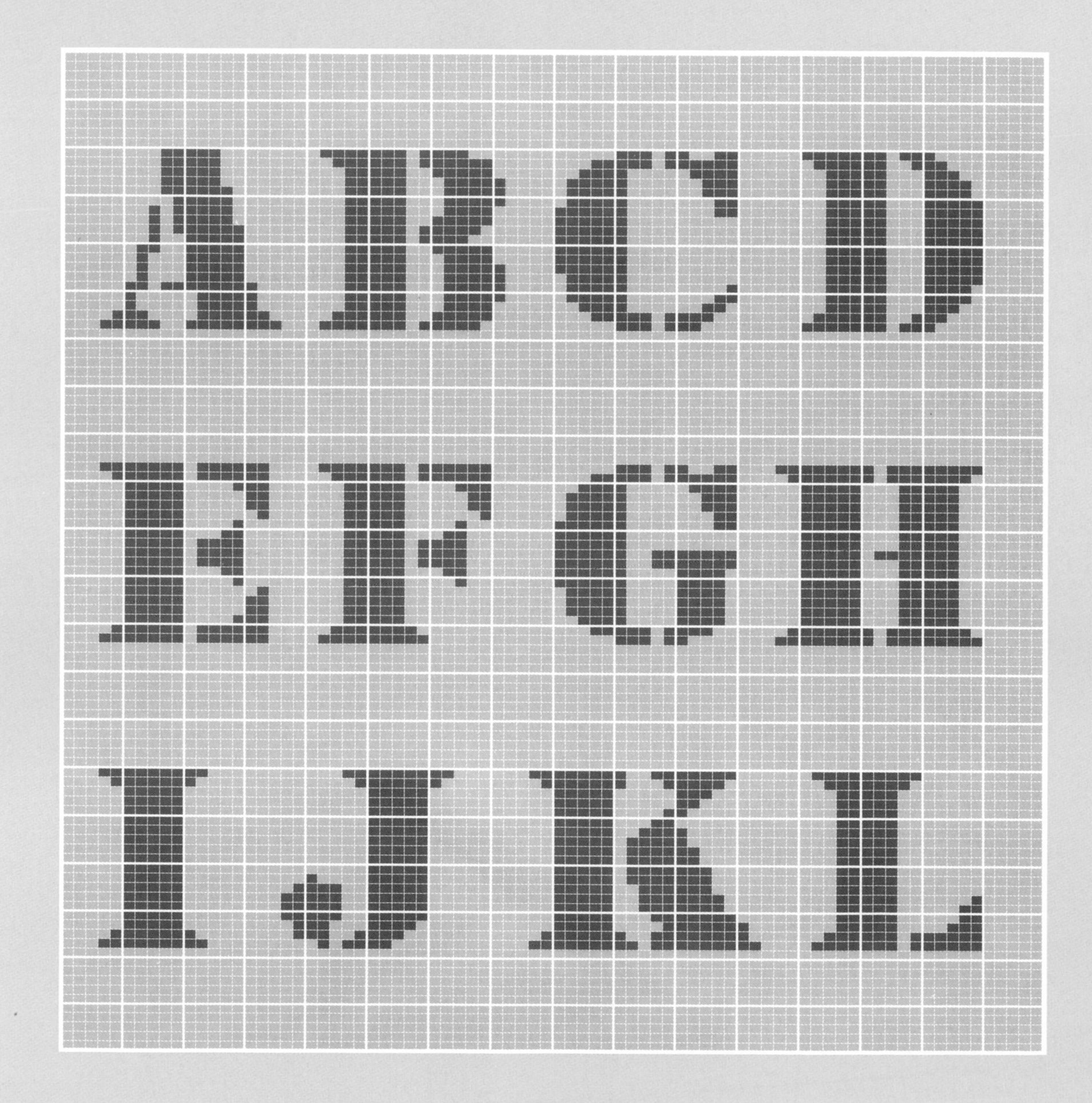

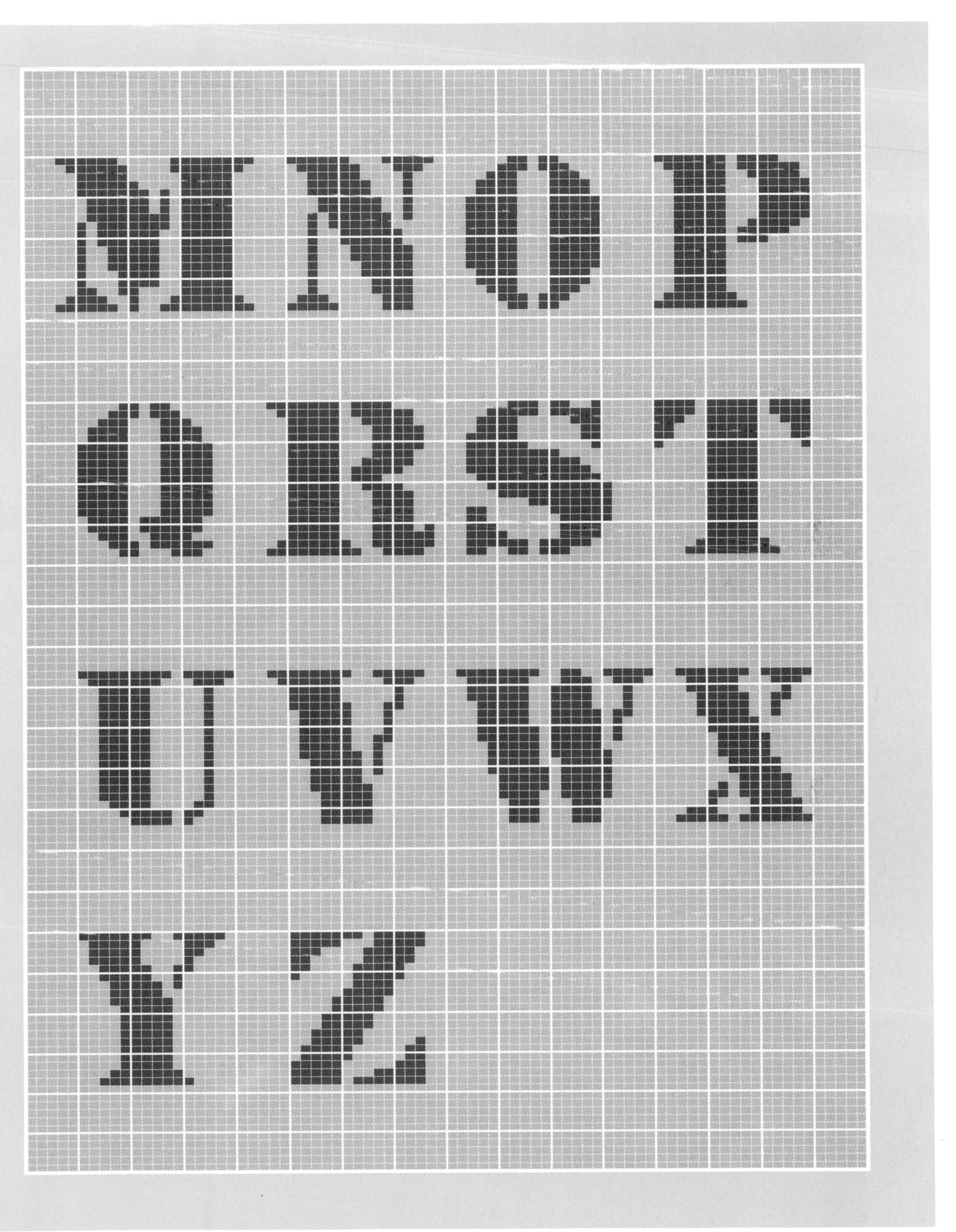

Script Uppercase Charts

(adapted from English typeface)

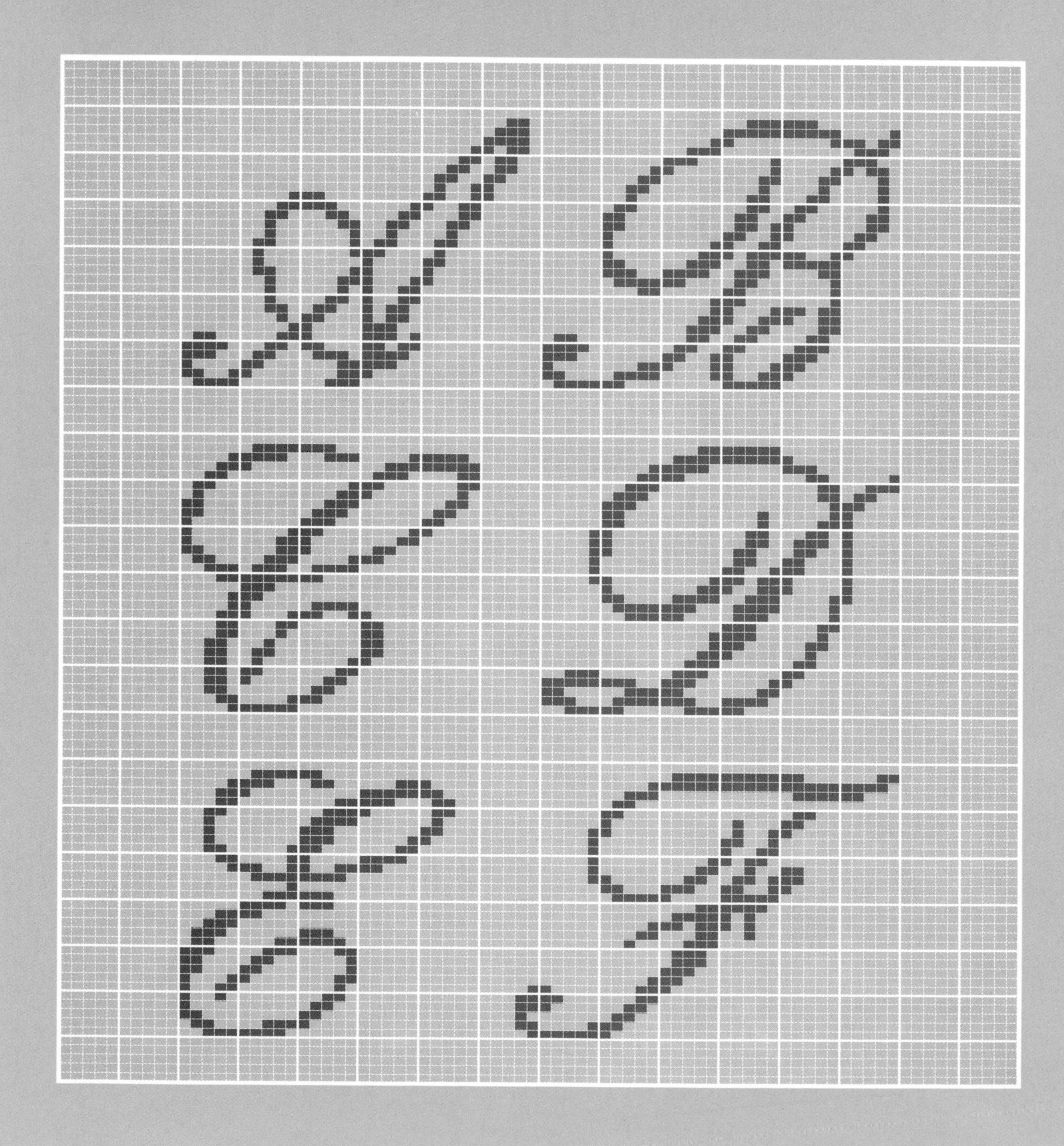

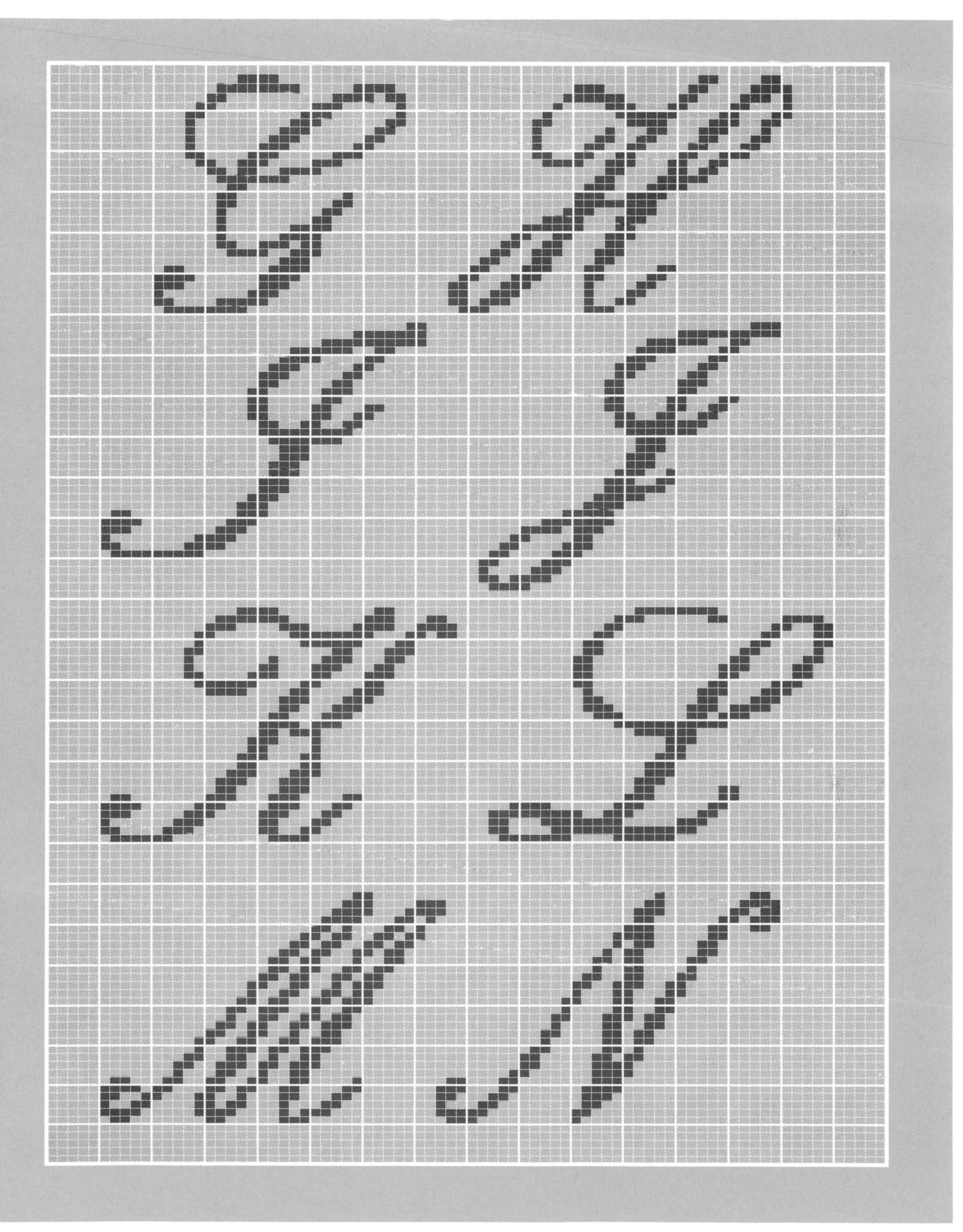

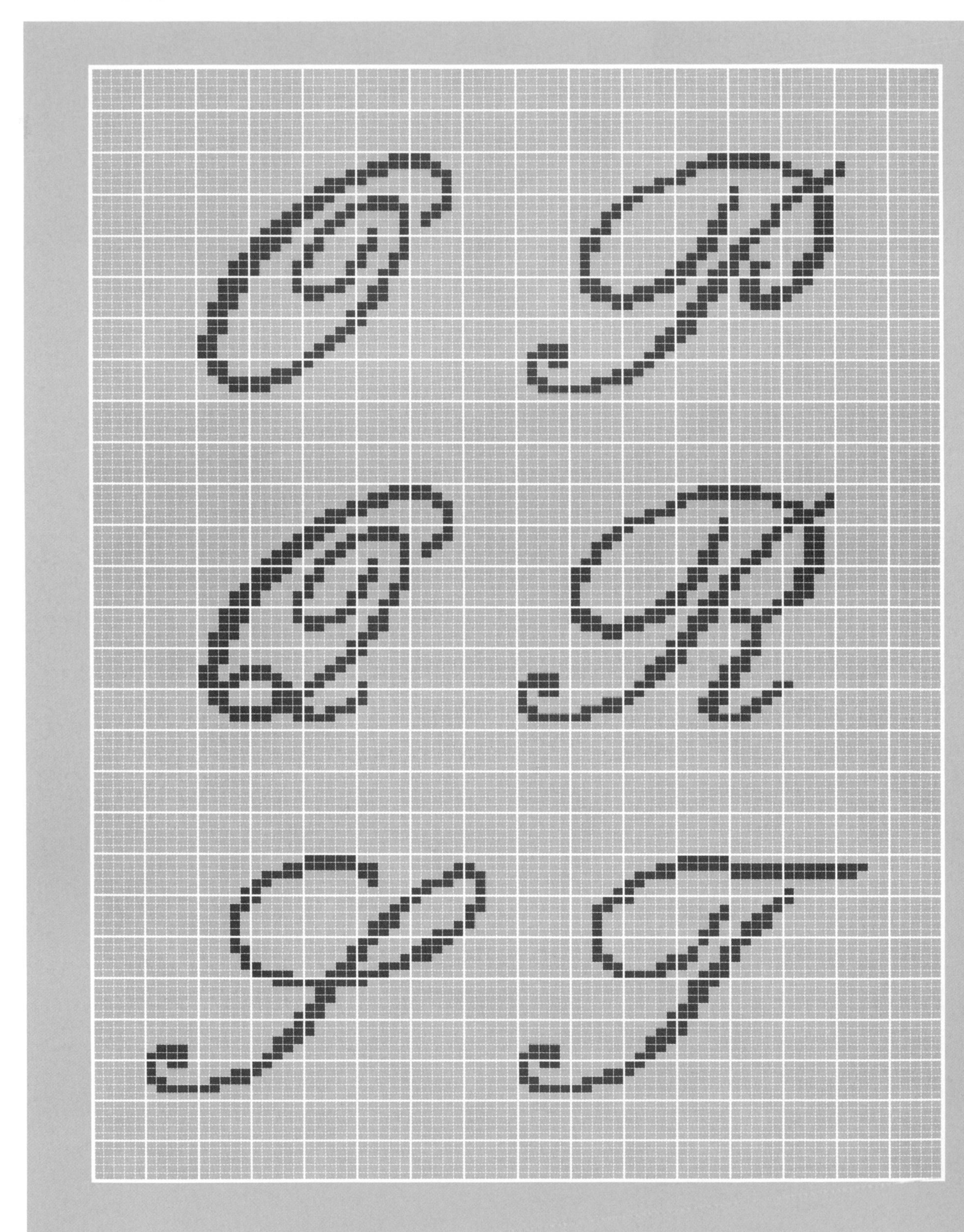

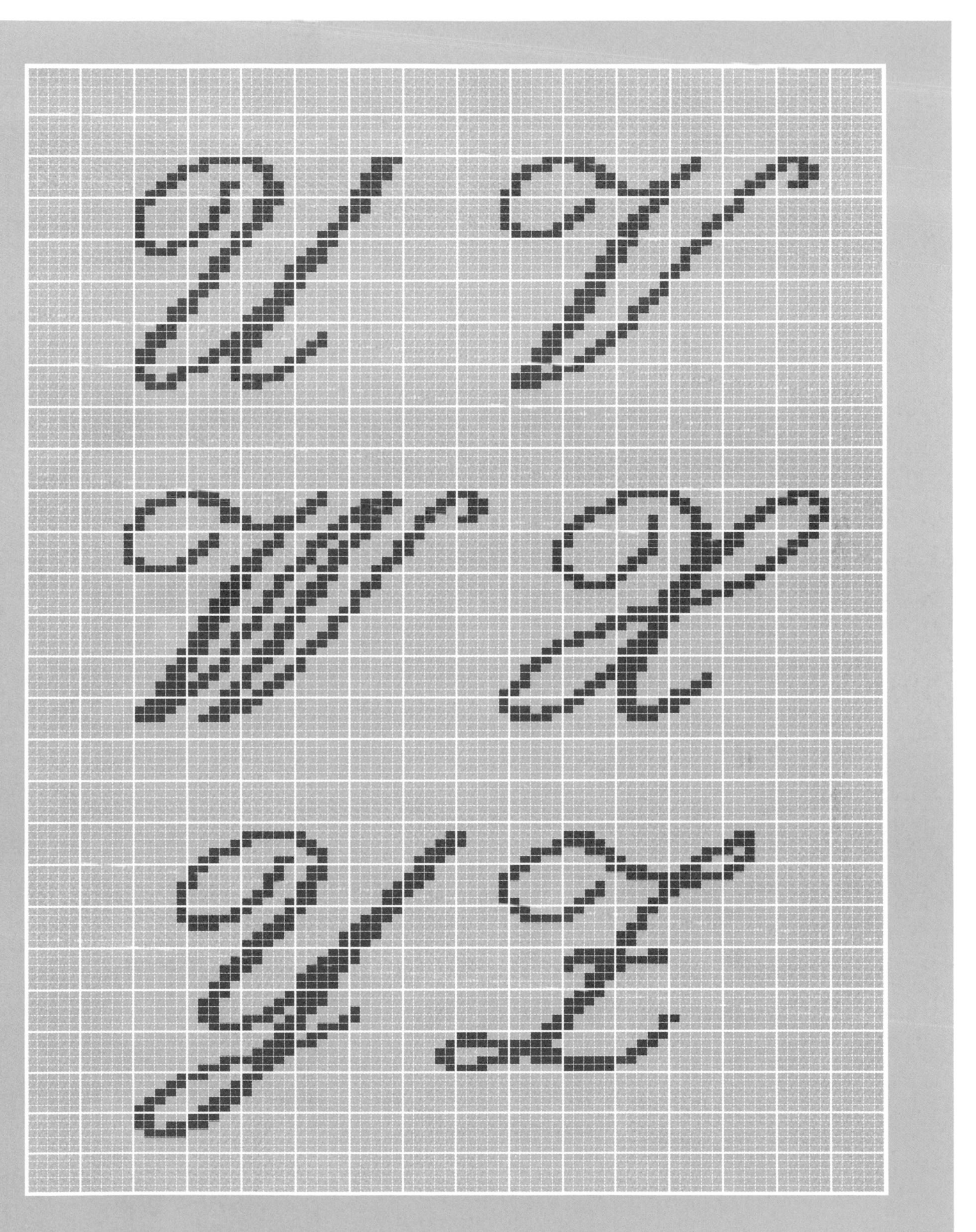

Script Lowercase Charts

(adapted from English typeface)

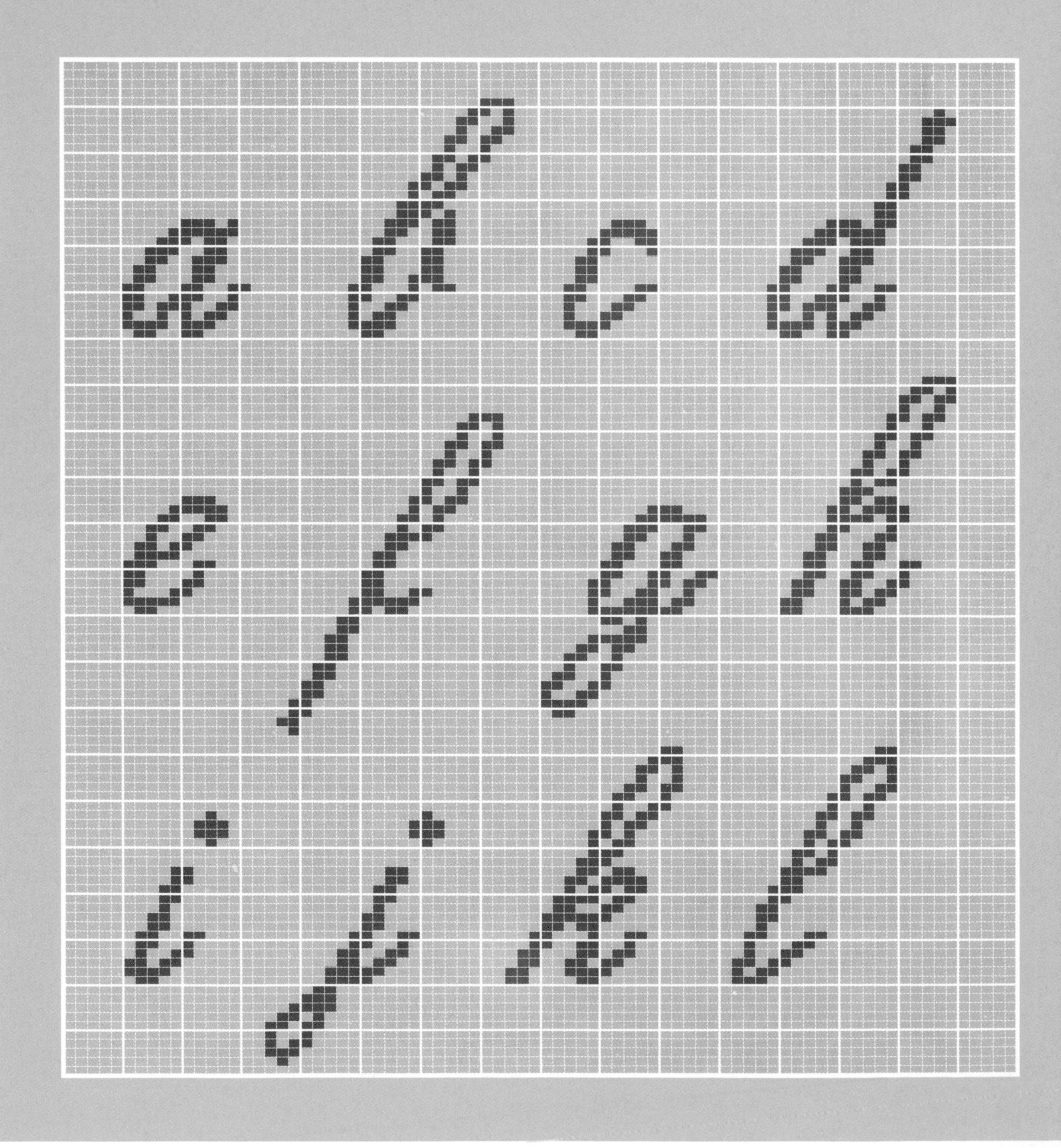

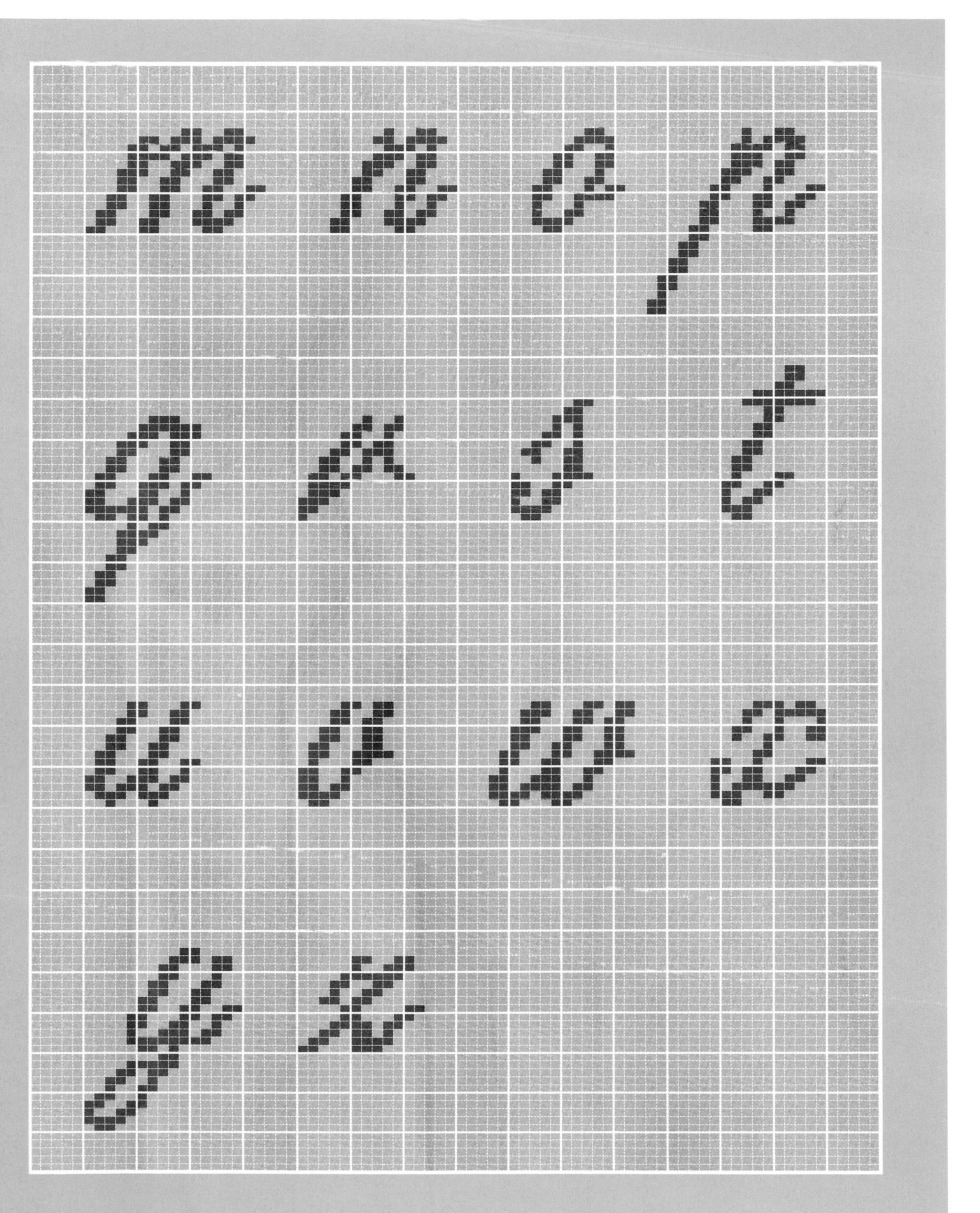

Circus Charts

(adapted from Coffee Tin typeface)

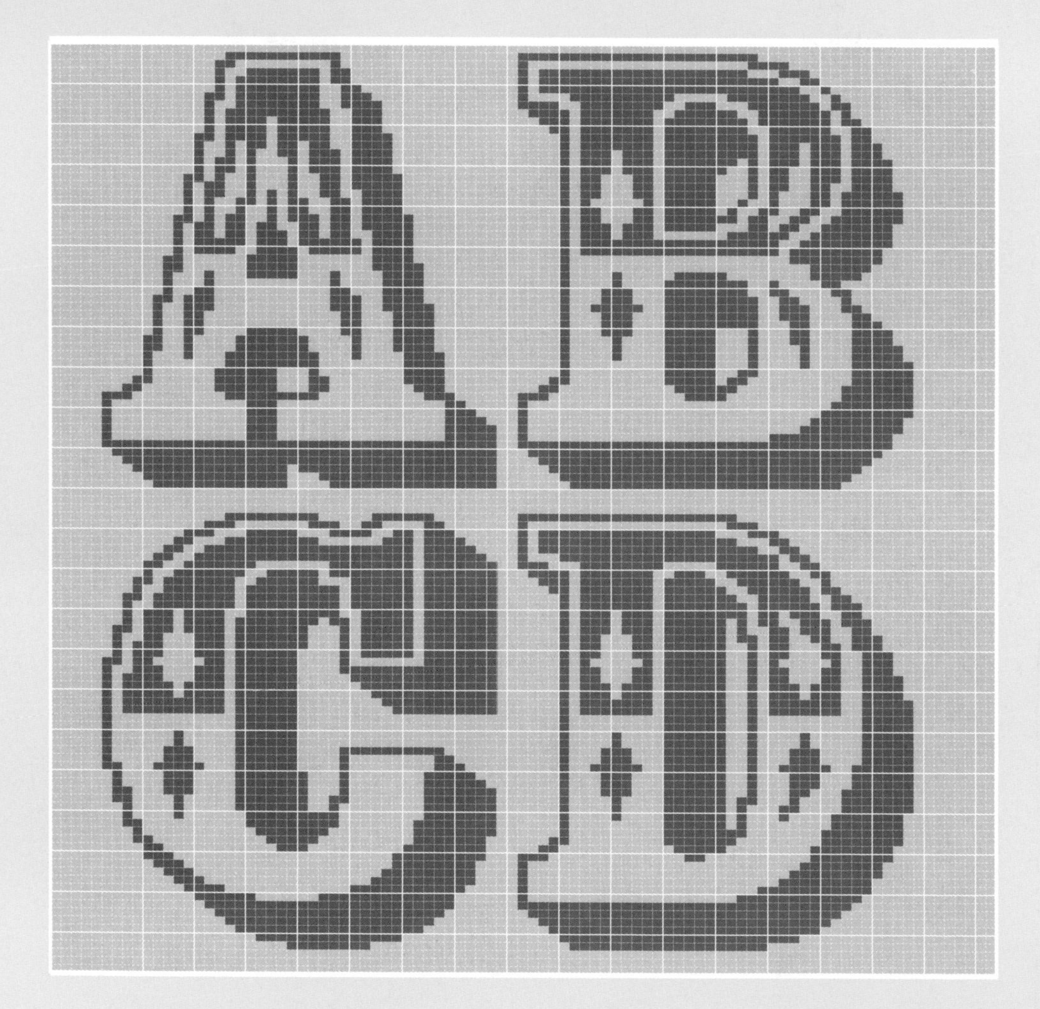

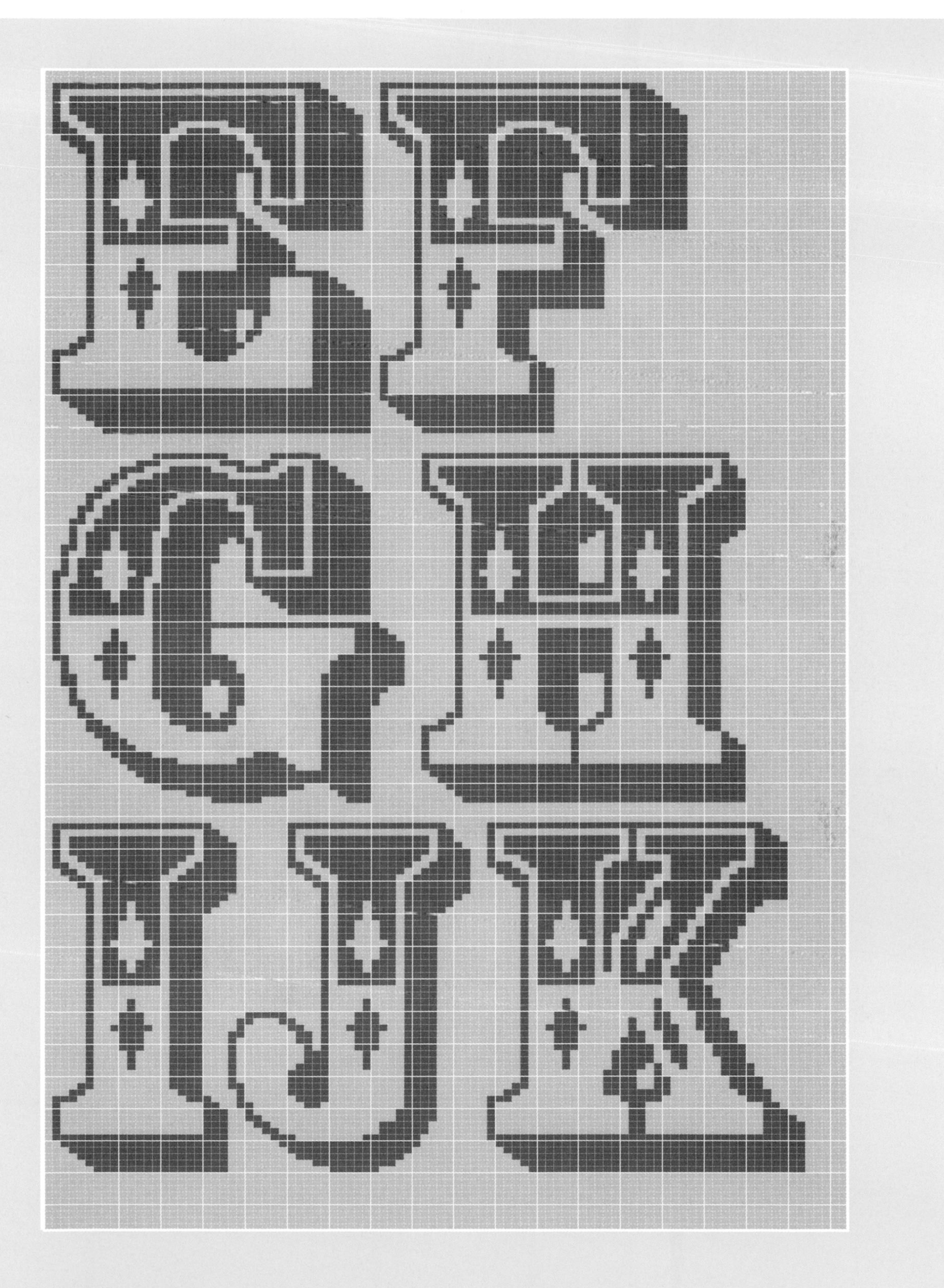

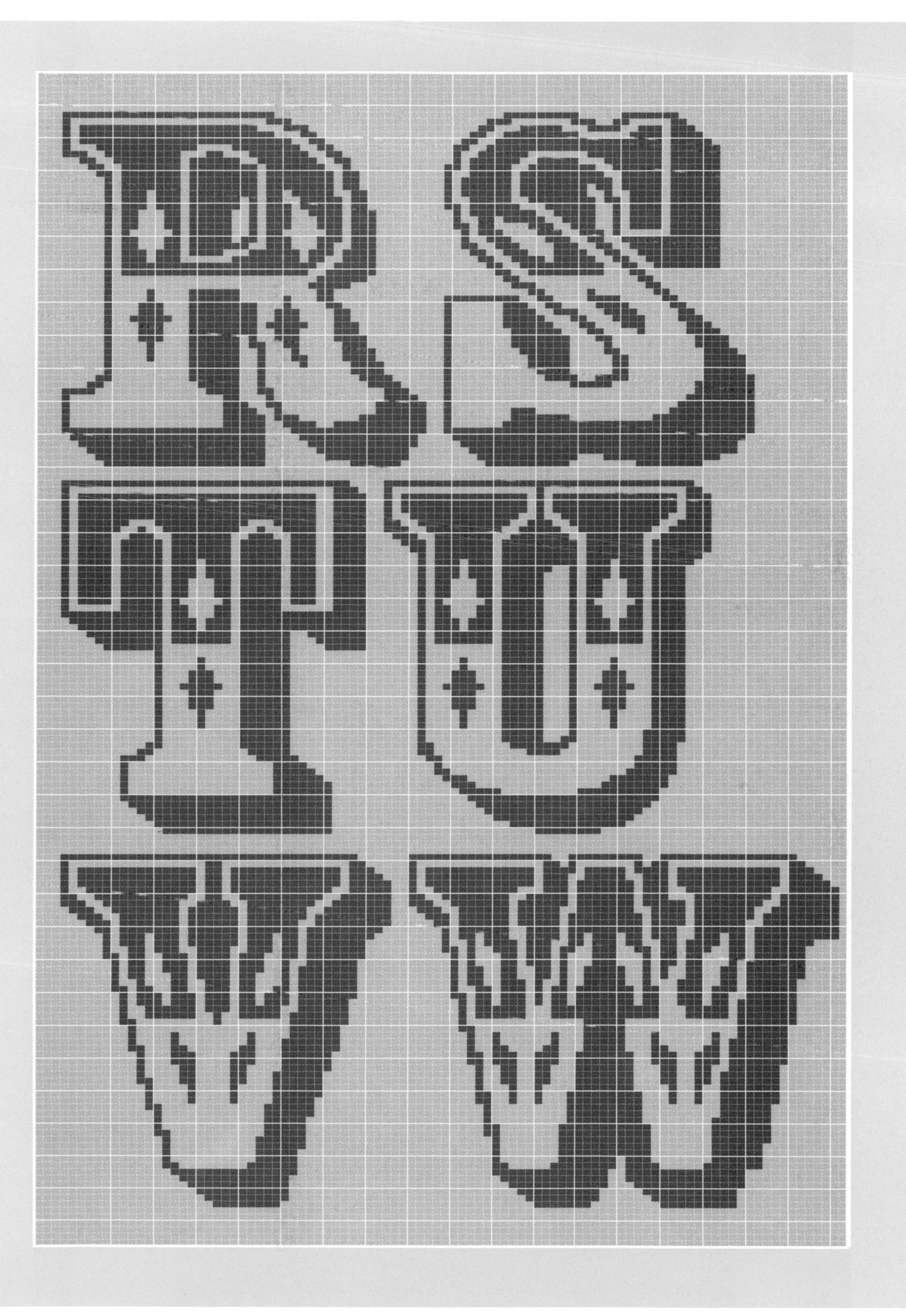

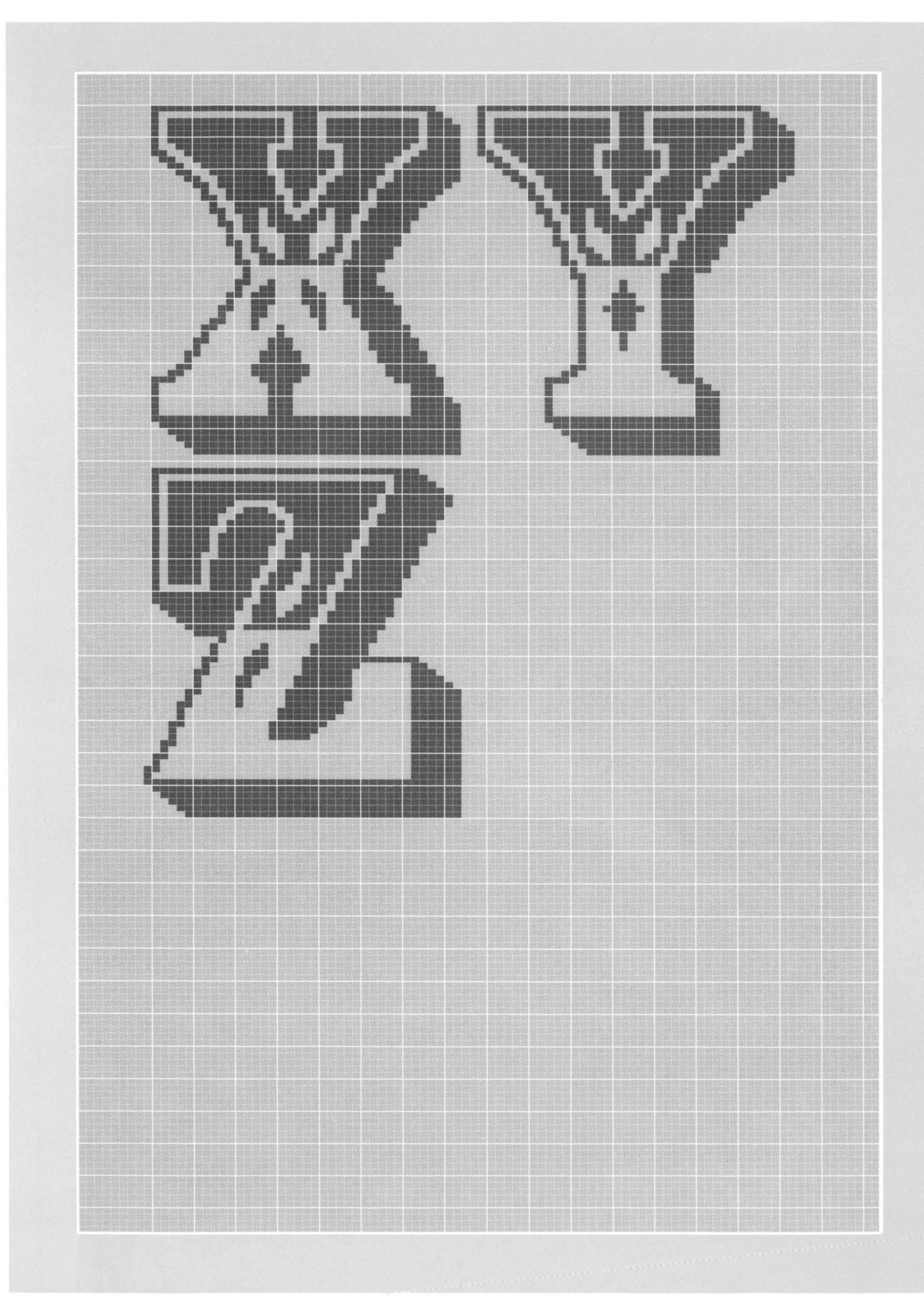

Western Charts

(adapted from Rio Oro typeface)

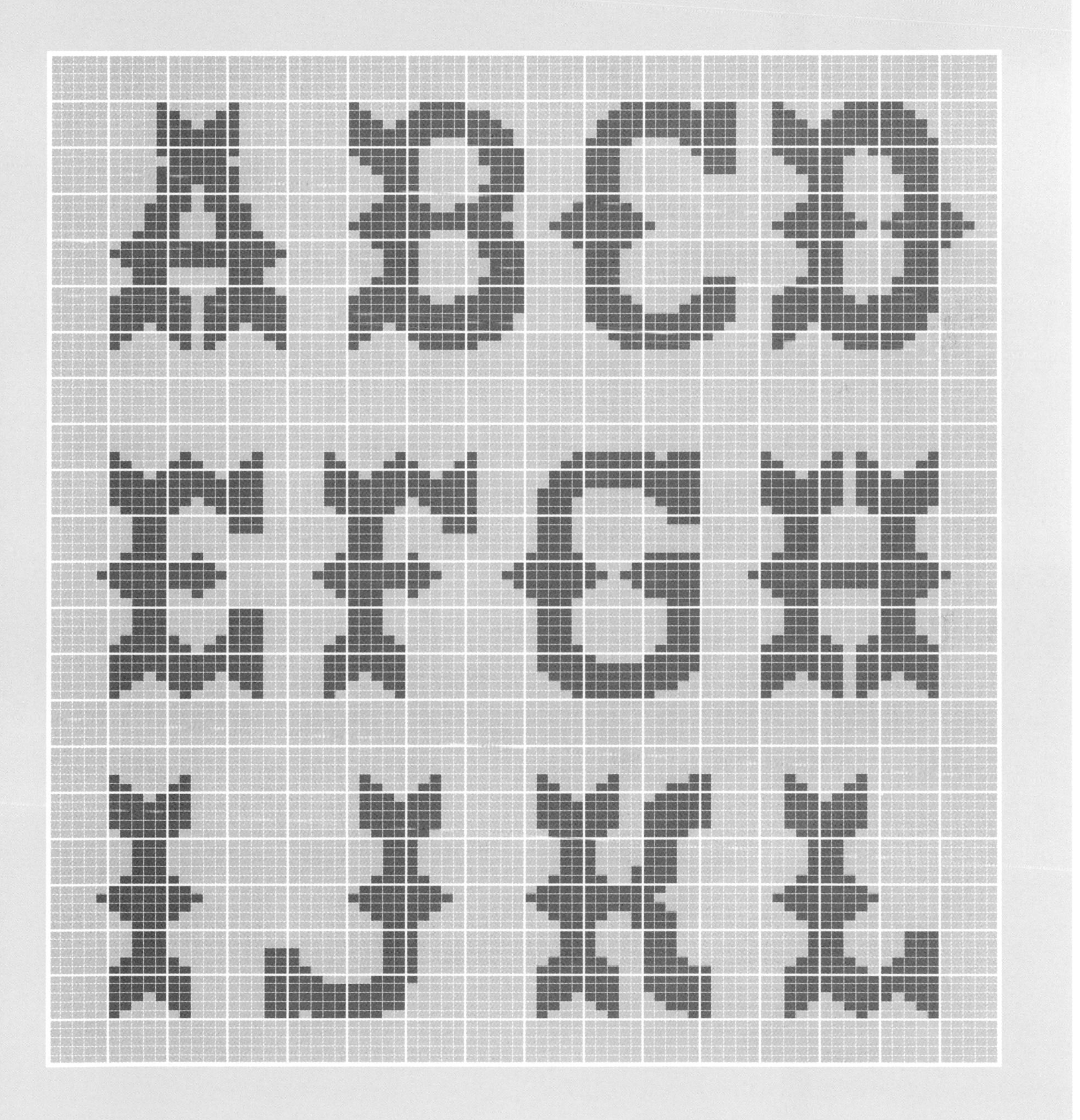

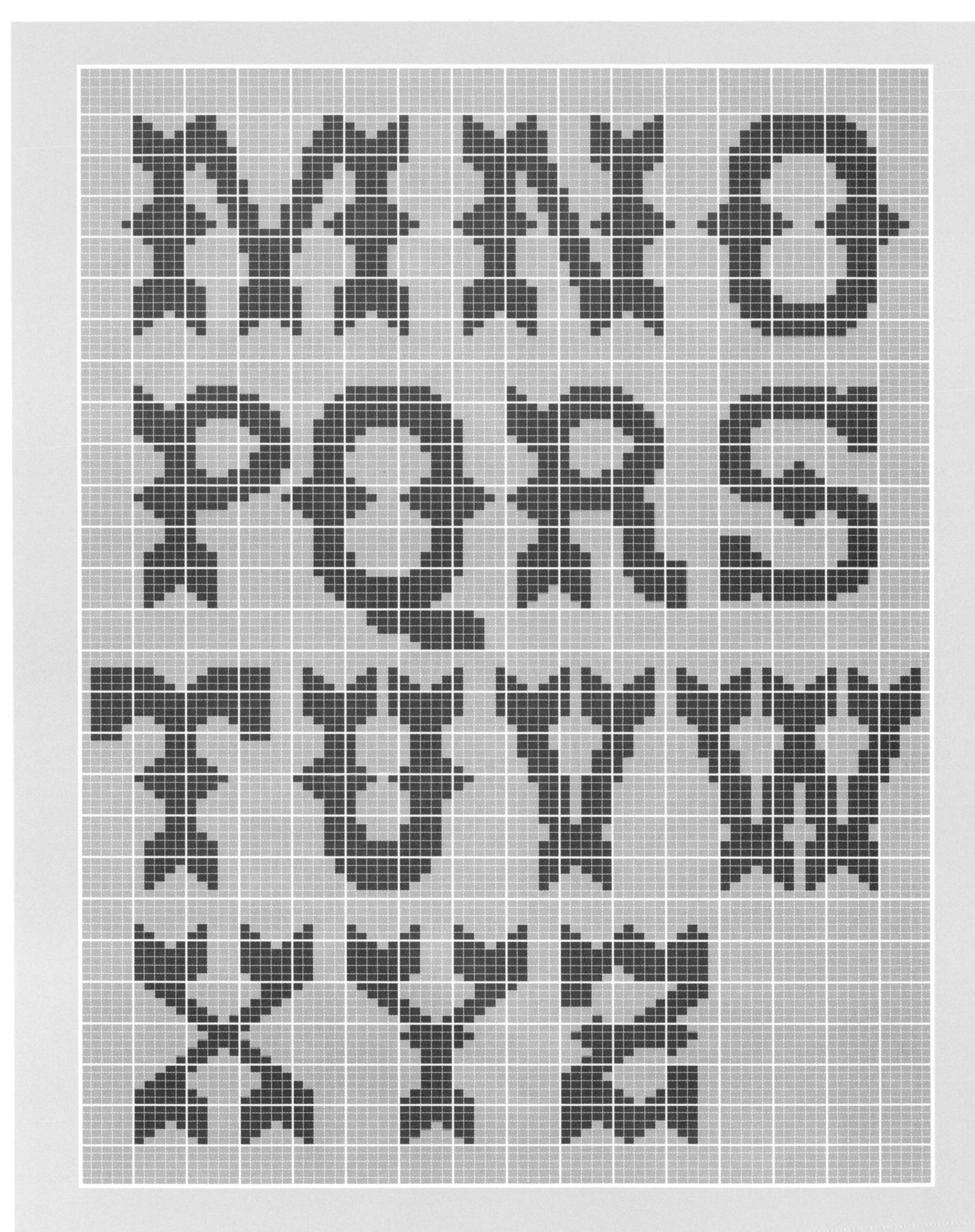

Black Letter Uppercase Charts

(adapted from Fette Fraktur typeface)

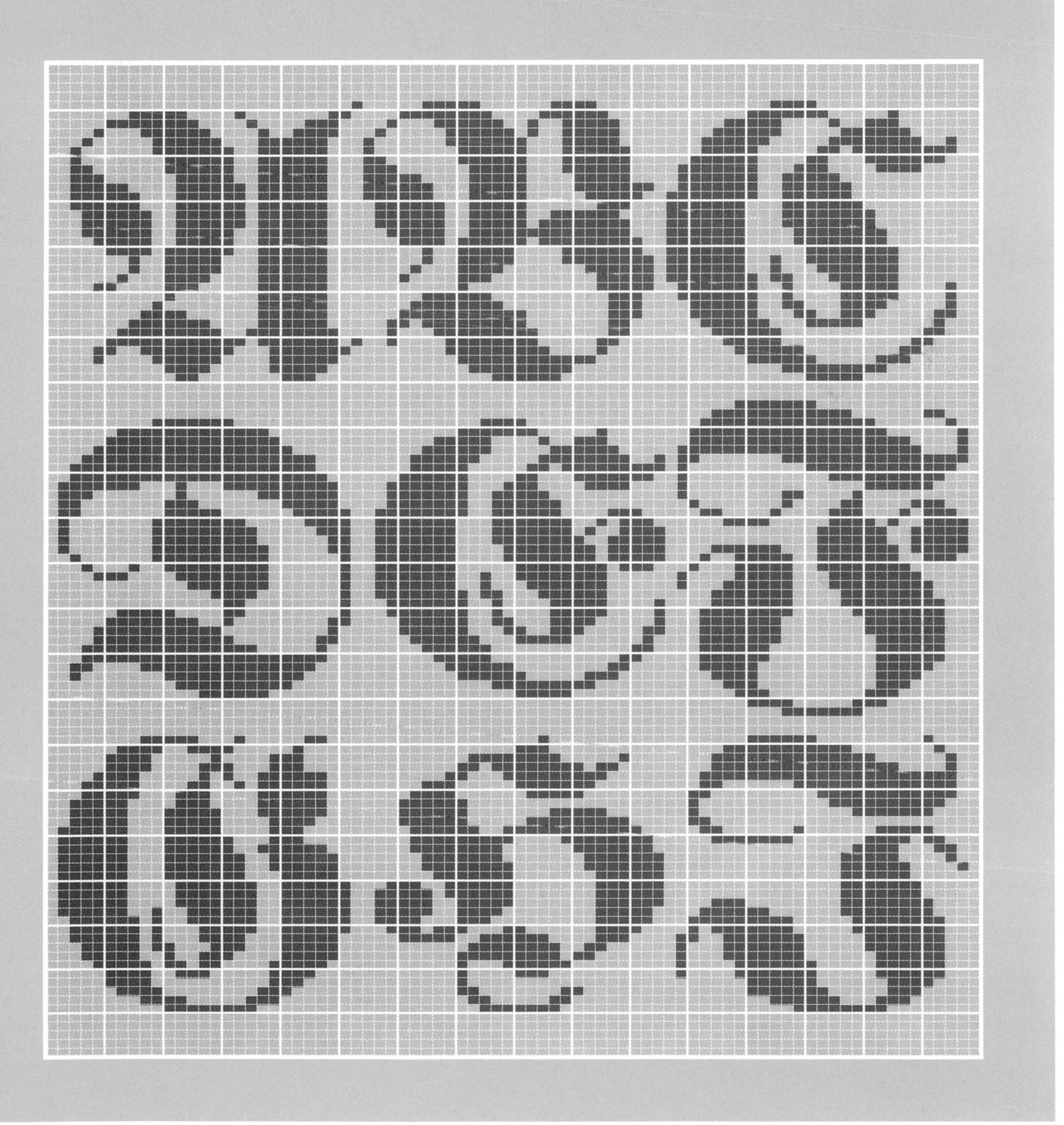

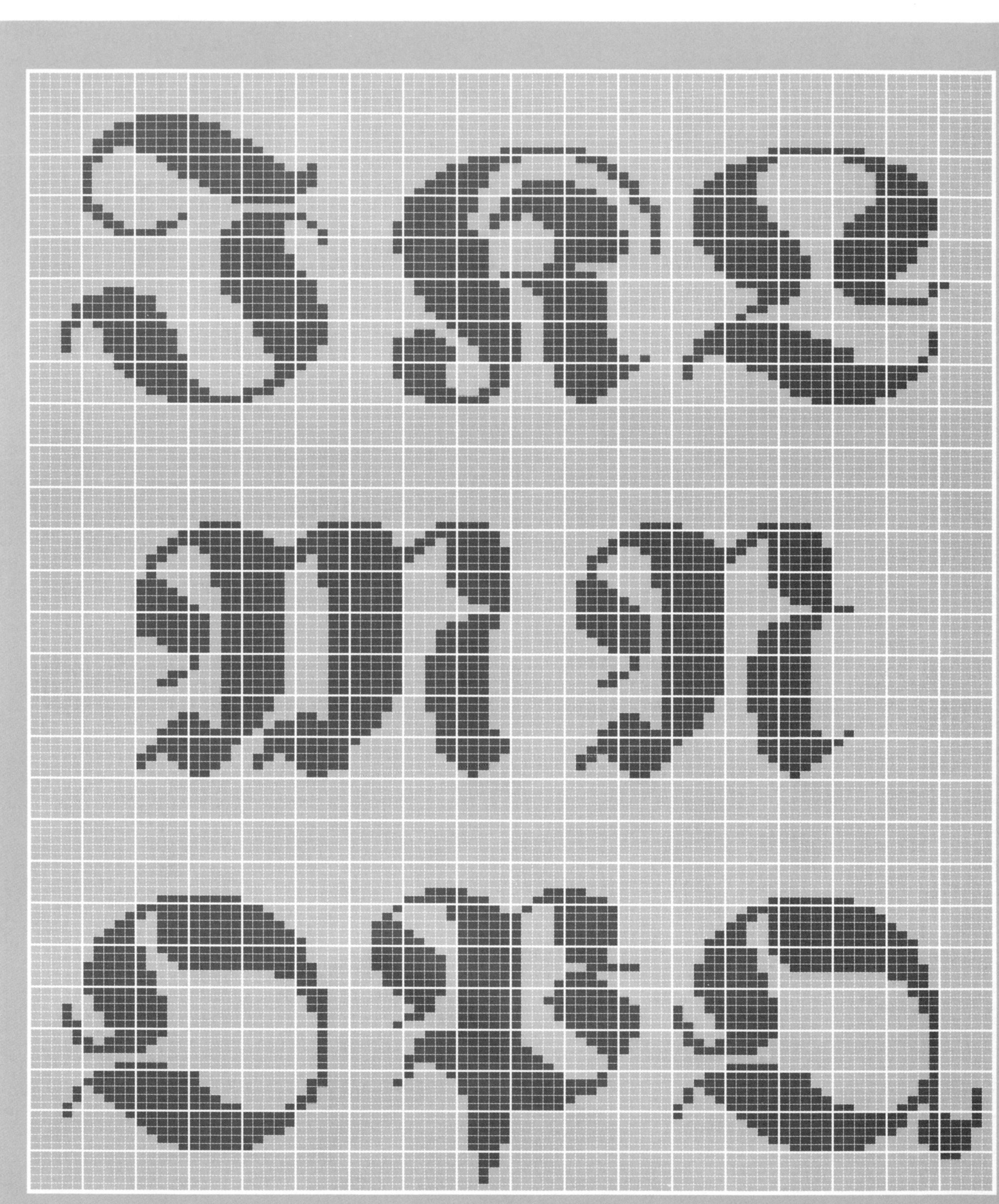

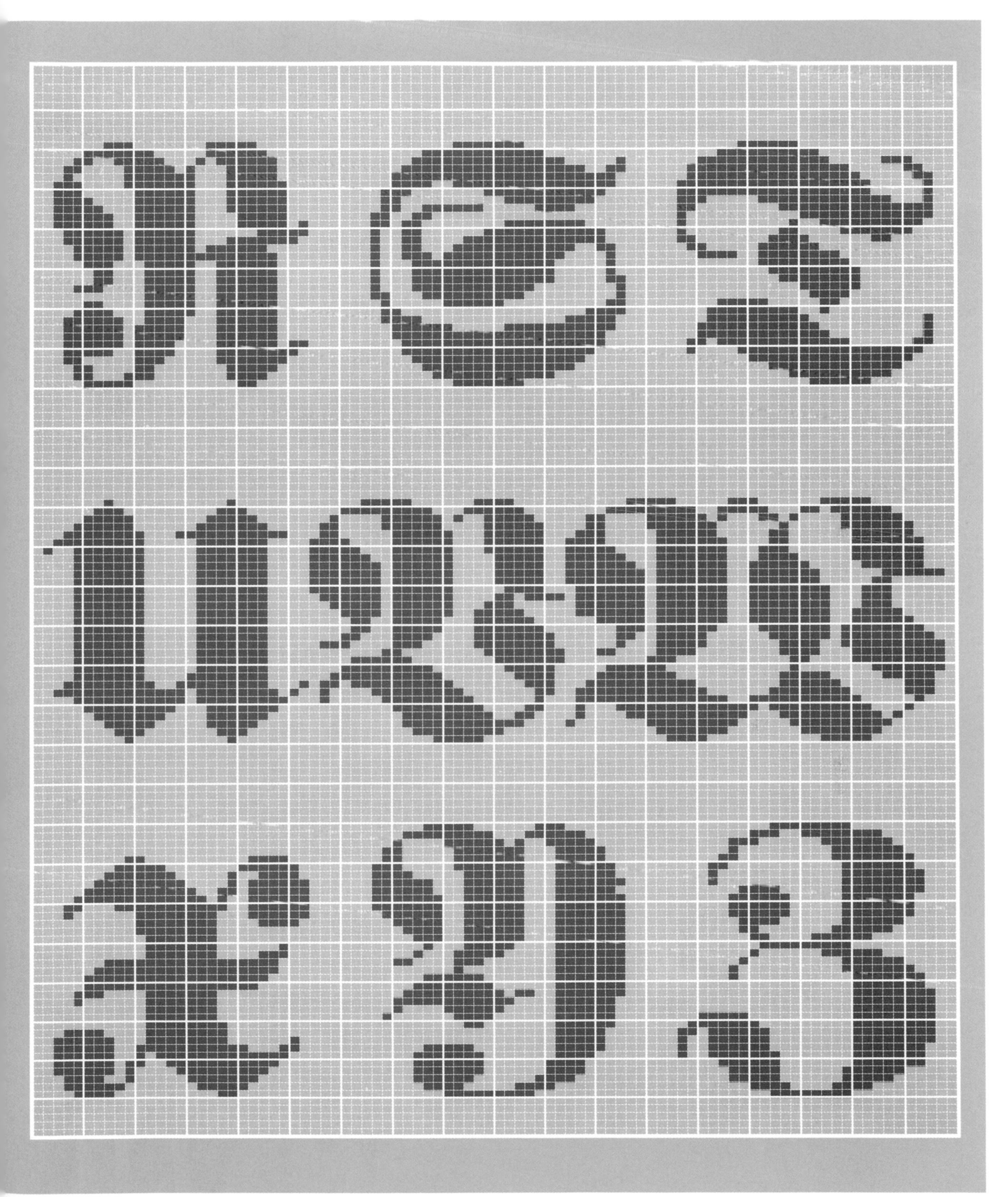

Black Letter Lowercase Charts

(adapted from Fette Fraktur typeface)

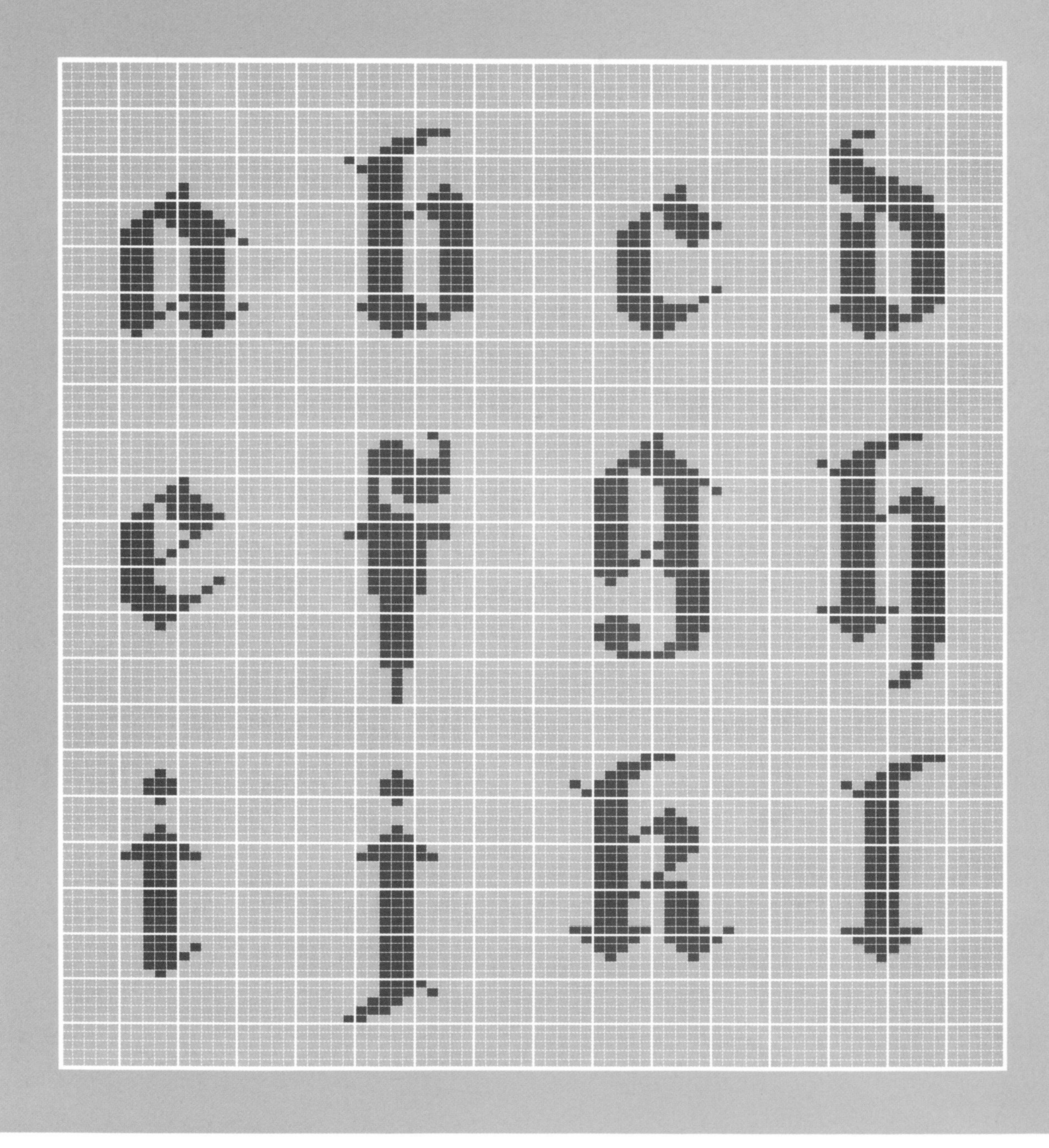

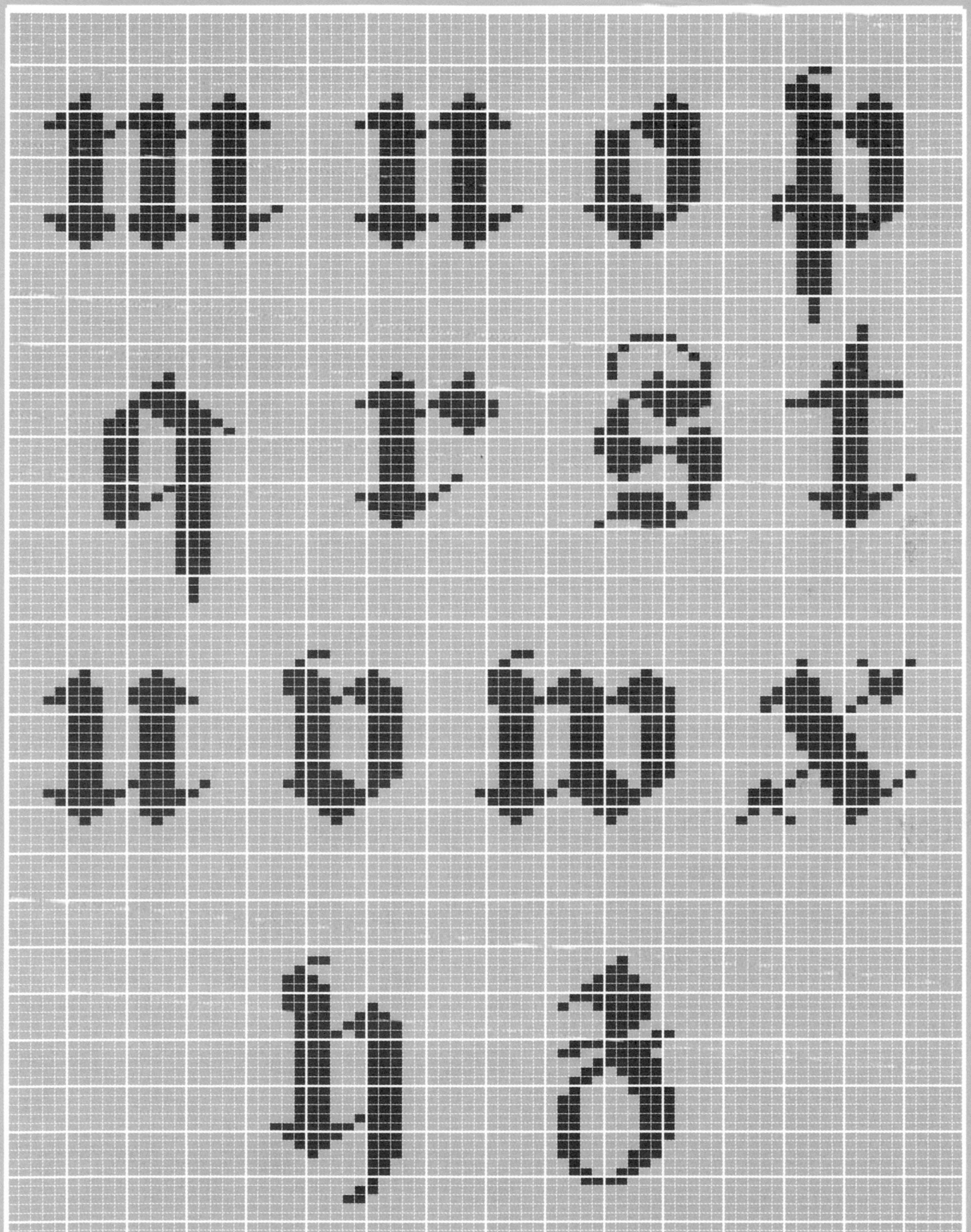

Numbers and Punctuation Charts

(adapted from Monaco typeface)

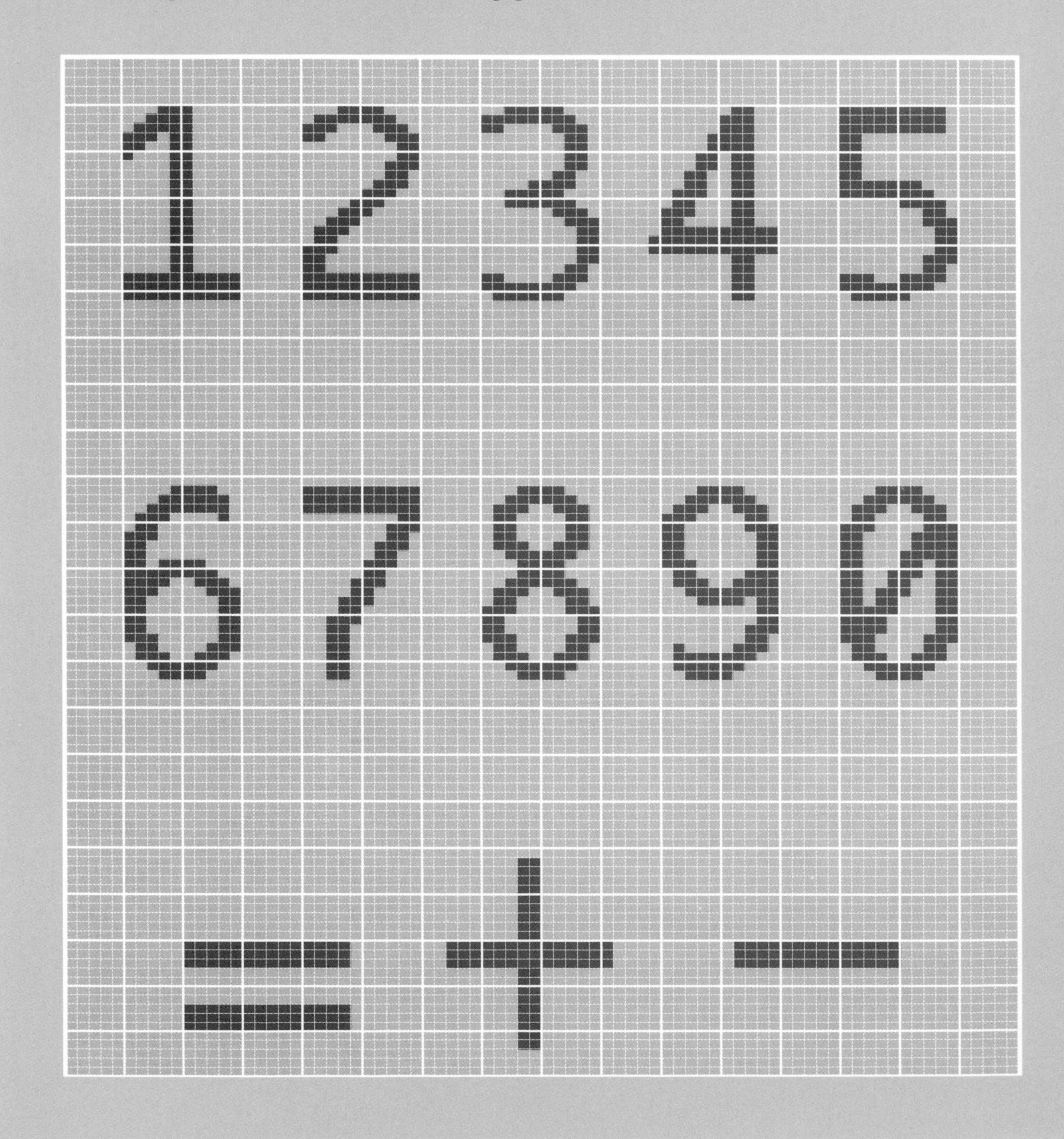

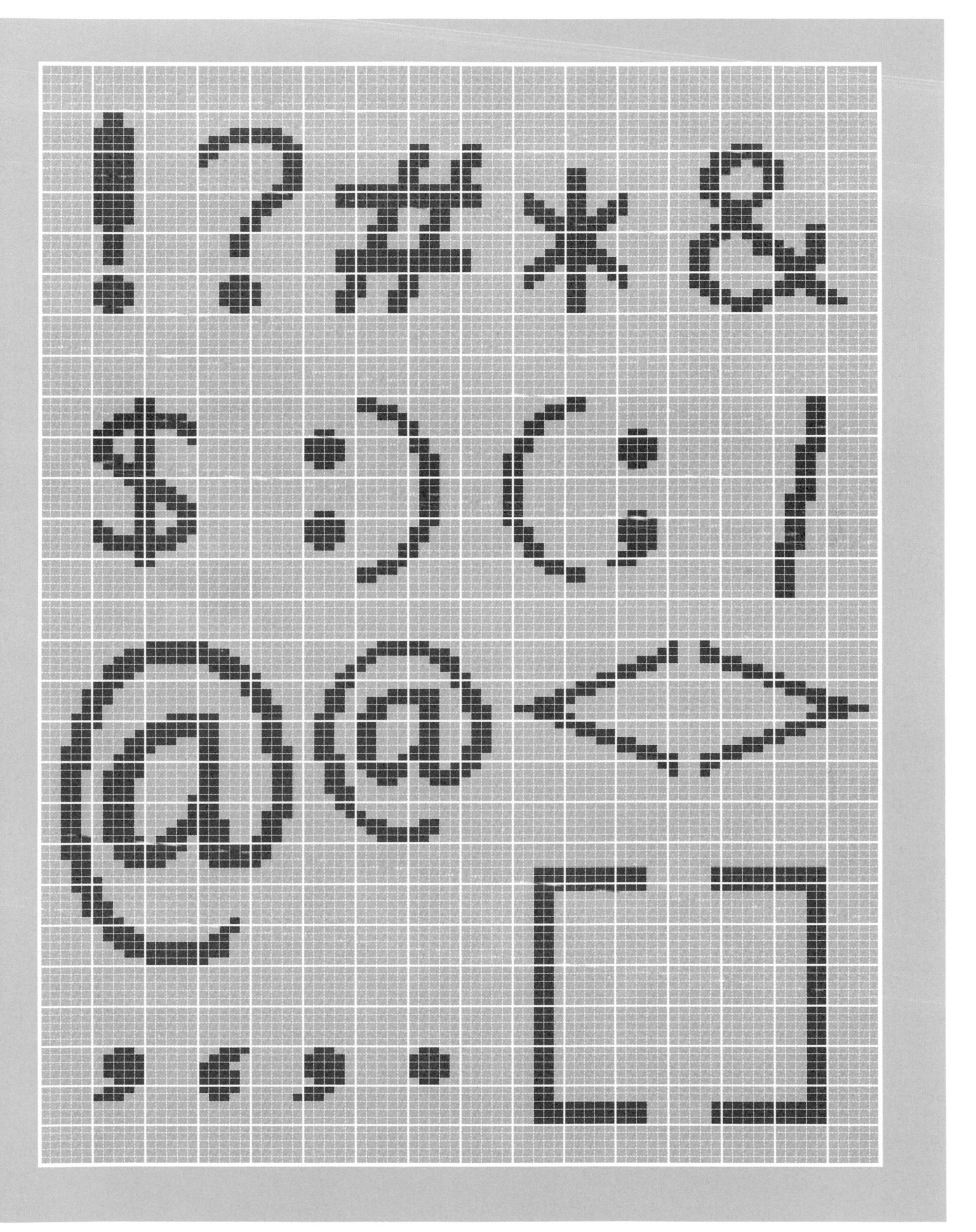

Index

Acknowledgments

The projects featured in this book were designed and knitted by the following designers:

Catherine Hirst
"STOP" Sign Doorstop (page 29)
"CAFE" French Press Cozy (page 61)
"Amour" Heart Pillow (page 71)

Erssie Major
Alphabet Baby Blocks (design only) (page 49)

Claire Crompton
Alphabet Pillow (page 25)
Letter Tile Coasters (page 32)
"Domus dulcis Domus" Wall Art (page 43)
Bookstore Tote (page 47)
Letterman Sweater (page 57)
Toy Tidy Bag (page 65)

Carol Meldrum
Felted Pencil Case (page 35)
"Ciao" Mittens (page 39)
Lady's "PARIS" Sweater (page 67)
Girl's Dress (page 75)
Mobius Twist Scarf (page 78)
Neckerchief (page 84)
"Carpe Diem" Covered Bracelets (page 92)
Wedding Pillow (page 95)

Liz Gregory
A–Z Bookends (page 99)
"LOVE" 3-D Letter Pillows (page 103)
Alphabet Baby Blocks (knitting only) (page 49)

Meghan Fernandes
Child's Initialed Backpack (page 53)
Baby Blanket (page 81)
"Ex Libris" E-reader Cover (page 87)
Black Letter Beanie (page 90)

Quintet Publishing would like to thank: the models, Danielle Holbrook, Carolina Connor, Luke Connor, and Joshua Tian Medina; Jane Cumberbatch for the photography location; BC Garn, DMC, Jamieson's, King Cole, Rico Design, Rowan, and Sirdar for supplying their excellent yarns for the various projects; Rachel Atkinson for her meticulous technical edit; Fred Brin for pattern-checking each of the projects; Lindsay Kaubi for copy editing; Diana Craig for proof reading; Julie Brooke for her editorial input; and Lydia Evans for her beautiful photography.